I0311147

Learn French with Luc et Sophie, Level 1

A Story-based Scheme for Teaching French at Lower KS2

Barbara Scanes

For instructions on how to download your free digital files, please see page 96.

We hope you enjoy using this book. If you would like further information on other books or e-resources published by Brilliant Publications, please write to the address given below or look on our website: www.brilliantpublications.co.uk.

Also available
Luc et Sophie French Stories for Primary Schools, Levels 1–4
Learn French with Luc et Sophie, Levels 2-4

Other books published by Brilliant Publications for teaching French

- 12 Mini French Plays
- 100+ Fun Ideas for Teaching French across the Curriculum
- 21 Fun Songs to Teach French Phonics
- Bonne Idée
- Brilliant French Information Books
- Brilliant Songs to Teach French Grammar
- C'est Français
- Chantez Plus Fort
- French Festivals and Traditions
- French Pen Pals Made Easy
- French Speaking Activities
- Fun French Fairy Tale Plays
- Getting to Grips with French Grammar at KS2
- J'aime Beaucoup Chanter en Français
- J'aime Chanter
- J'aime Parler
- Jouez, Dansez et Apprenez le Français
- Jouons Tous Ensemble
- Loto Français
- Petites Étoiles
- Physical French Phonics
- Unforgettable French

Published by Brilliant Publications Limited
Unit 10
Sparrow Hall Farm
Edlesborough
Dunstable
Bedfordshire
LU6 2ES, UK

E-mail: info@brilliantpublications.co.uk
Website: www.brilliantpublications.co.uk
Tel: 01525 222292

The name Brilliant Publications is a registered trademark.

Written by Barbara Scanes
Illustrated by Paul Hutchinson
Songs and audio files produced by Hart McLeod

© Text Barbara Scanes 2014, revised 2019 and 2025
© Design Brilliant Publications Limited 2014, revised 2019 and 2025

ISBN printed book: 978-1-78317-390-7
ISBN PDF book: 978-1-78317-394-5

First printed in the UK with the title 'Learn French with Luc et Sophie, 1ère Partie' in 2014; reprinted 2016, 2019. This revised edition printed 2025.

The right of Barbara Scanes to be identified as the author of this work has been asserted by herself in accordance with the Copyright, Designs and Patents Act 1988.

All rights reserved. Apart from any use permitted under UK copyright law, no part of this publication may be reproduced or transmitted in any form or by any means, electronic or mechanical, including photocopying and recording, or held within any information storage and retrieval system, without permission in writing from the publishers or under licence from the Copyright Licensing Agency Limited. Further details of such licenses (for reprographic reproduction) may be obtained from the Copyright Licensing Agency Limited, 5th Floor, Shackleton House, 4 Battle Bridge Lane, London SE1 2HX (https://cla.co.uk).

Contents

	Page
Introduction	4
What's in this resource?	5
How to Use this book	7
Topics/grammar in each unit	10
Progression through the series	11

Unité 1	Bonjour	15
Unité 2	Je m'appelle Sophie	23
Unité 3	Combien de biscuits ?	34
Unité 4	J'ai six ans	46
Unité 5	J'ai un frère	55
Unité 6	Beaucoup de bonbons	65
Unité 7	Un bonbon rouge	76

Traductions des chansons (Song translations)	88
Instructions utiles (Useful commands)	89
Les téléchargements numériques (Digital downloads)	90
Vocabulaire (Vocabulary)	92
Solutions (Answers)	95
Instructions for downloading the digital files	96

Introduction

Learn French with Luc et Sophie is a story-based approach to teaching French at Key Stage 2, divided into four levels.

Learn French with Luc et Sophie will not only provide you with 28 specially written French storybooks, it will also provide you with a wealth of creative teaching ideas to ensure complete coverage of the Foreign Language Programmes of Study in the September 2014 National Curriculum for England. The scheme is designed with non-specialists in mind and will make implementing the National Curriculum easy.

There are seven stories in **Learn French with Luc et Sophie, Level 1**. Children will love diving into these humorous French tales, specially created to inspire and motivate young learners. Written in simple, everyday language, the stories provide a fantastic introduction to French, making it easy and enjoyable for children to start learning.

Tried and tested in a variety of primary classrooms, these stories are a hit with children. They'll be drawn to the colourful illustrations of Luc, Sophie and their lively friends and family—and eager to find out what happens next! Like most siblings, Luc and Sophie have their moments of sibling rivalry, adding a relatable and entertaining touch.

The language structures and vocabulary in the stories have been carefully chosen so you can be sure that they are appropriate for use with beginning learners. Pupils will be able to use the language they learn in real life conversations.

The stories link to topics often taught in primary schools such as common greetings, asking and saying one's name and age, family members, numbers to 20 and colours, so it is easy to use them as the basis for your French curriculum or integrate them with any other primary French scheme.

What's in this resource?

This book contains lesson plans for each of the units, providing ideas for developing pupils' speaking, listening, writing and reading skills. As the time available and the pace at which pupils can work will differ from school to school and class to class, we haven't provided rigid lesson plans. There is ample material in each unit for 2–3 lessons.

Lists of vocabulary used in the stories and lessons

Exercises, games and activities linked to the stories

Translations of the stories

Helpful background grammar information for teachers

Printable worksheets

Song lyrics

Script versions of the stories to enable pupils to act them out

Self-assessment (*Je peux …*) sheets for each unit

Learn French with Luc et Sophie, Level 1
© Barbara Scanes and Brilliant Publications Limited

Free digital downloads

The free digital downloads provide you with all the resources to introduce the stories and teach French successfully. Please see pages 90–91 for the file names.

Audio enhanced e-storybooks

The seven stories in Level 1 are provided as audio enhanced e-storybooks for display on the Interactive Whiteboard for shared reading.

Click on the speech bubbles to hear native speakers acting out the stories.

Click on the individual words and phrases in the *Vocabulaire* list to hear them being spoken.

Audio files

The track numbers for the audio files are listed on pages 90–91. They contain:
- songs sung by native French speakers
- instrumental versions of the songs
- audio files for all the stories, acted out by native French speakers
- vocabulary lists, modelling all the vocabulary used in the units
- listening exercises

Printable resources

PDF versions of the stories are provided so that you can print them out and share them with your class. PDF versions of the worksheets, assessment sheets, song lyrics and mini play scripts are also provided to make printing them out easier.

The seven Level 1 stories are also available for purchase separately as an anthology, which is available as both a printed book and a PDF.

Luc et Sophie French Stories for Primary Schools, Level 1
ISBN printed book   978-1-78317-382-2
ISBN PDF   978-1-78317-386-0

How to use this book

Structure of each unit
We recommend that you follow a similar structure when teaching each unit.

Cinq minutes français
We recommend that you start each unit (apart from the first one) with *Cinq minutes français* – five minutes of French. Use gestures to help communicate and don't worry about using the occasional English word or phrase. When both you and your pupils are more familiar with the vocabulary, it will be easier and more natural for you to conduct the entire *Cinq minutes français* in French.

A list of useful commands is provided on page 89 and on tracks 46 (for plural/formal commands) and 47 (for singular/informal commands).

'Blind' listening exercise
Listen to the story on its own first, and encourage pupils to infer as much meaning as possible from the cognates and vocabulary introduced in previous units.

Listening and reading exercise
Display the audio enhanced e-storybook on the IWB. Click on the speech bubbles to hear what the characters are saying. Brainstorm the meaning of the entire story as a class-wide exercise, using cognates and pictures as clues. Alternatively, listen to the story again and follow along with the text using the printed storybook. For the longer stories, you may want to break the story down into chunks.

Reading aloud and acting out
Reading the story aloud and then acting it out will help to practise the vocabulary orally and to familiarise the pupils with the sounds of the words in French. The stories are also presented as *Petites pièces* (mini-scripts) to enable them to be acted out.

Creating own stories and mini role plays
Pupils should be encouraged to use the vocabulary and sentence structures in the stories to create their own stories and mini role plays. This will help them to internalise the language and build their confidence, making them feel they can speak French.

Song
For each unit there is a song that reinforces the vocabulary used in the story. The lyrics of the song are given on a photocopiable sheet. As part of the digitial downloads, you will find audio recordings of the songs, sung by native French speakers, and an instrumental version to enable 'karaoke' performances. Occasionally the songs introduce some new vocabulary (*Vocabulaire supplémentaire*). Where this happens you will find the new vocabulary listed in *Vocabulaire pour le professeur*, along with an audio file.

Other exercises

Other exercises will be topic-specific but will also recur from time to time in other chapters. The mixture of exercises has been planned to ensure pupils practise all four skills, which are indicated using the following logos:

 reading    writing   speaking    listening

Worksheets (Feuilles de travail)

For each unit there are worksheets to reinforce the vocabulary/grammar learnt in the unit.

Vocabulary

The vocabulary builds as you progress through the storybooks, with the stories reinforcing vocabulary and language structures already learned. All new vocabulary is listed in the storybooks, in the audio enhanced e-storybooks and in the relevant unit in the teacher's book. The vocabulary is spoken by a native speaker on an audio file and can be also heard by clicking on the *Vocabulaire* lists in the e-storybooks.

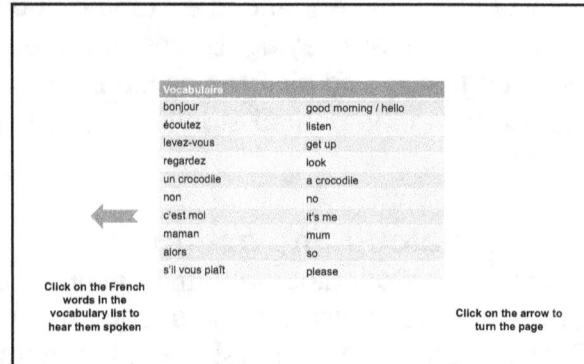

Where the stories use vocabulary introduced in previous units, the vocabulary has been listed as *Vocabulaire déjà utilisé* (under the *Vocabulaire* on the first page of each unit in the Teacher's book). A full list of the vocabulary introduced is on pages 92–94.

Where additional vocabulary (*Vocabulaire supplémentaire*) has been introduced (either in one of the *exercices* or in a song), the new words and phrases are included on the *Vocabulaire pour le professeur* list for that unit and on the relevant audio track.

The following vocabulary may also be useful:

French	English
activités pour le tableau blanc interactif (TBI)	activities for the interactive whiteboard (IWB)
la chanson	song
chanter	to sing
écouter	to listen
écrire	to write
l'exercice	exercise
la feuille de travail	worksheet
la grammaire	grammar
l'histoire	story

lire	to read
parler	to speak
la traduction de l'histoire	translation of the story
l'unité	unit
le vocabulaire	vocabulary
le Vocabulaire déjà utilisé	repeated vocabulary
le vocabulaire supplémentaire	additional vocabulary
le vocabulaire pour le professeur	vocabulary for the teacher

Topics/grammar in each unit

The following topics/grammar are introduced in each unit:

	Unité	Vocabulary focus	Grammar focus
1	Bonjour	*bonjour, s'il vous plaît*, simple commands	commands (imperative tense)
2	Je m'appelle Sophie	*au revoir*, asking and saying your name, asking and saying how you're feeling	subject pronouns: *je* and *tu*
3	Combien de biscuits ?	numbers 1–10, *j'ai, combien de?*	*avoir* (1st person singular), plurals
4	J'ai six ans	asking and saying your age	*avoir* (1st and 2nd person singular) when talking about age
5	J'ai un frère	family members (*frère, sœur*), *je voudrais* …	possessives
6	Beaucoup de bonbons	numbers 11–20	*avoir* (3rd person singular) – forming simple sentences
7	Un bonbon rouge	colours, more commands	colours as adjectives

Progression through the series

Learn French with Luc et Sophie has been written to ensure coverage of the National Curriculum for England Programmes of Study for Foreign Languages. The chart below shows what most children should be able to do by the end of each level. The Self-assessment sheets, with 'I can …' (*Je peux…*) statements, at the end of each unit will help you to assess pupils' progress.

National Curriculum programme of study	Level 1 outcome expectations	Level 2 outcome expectations	Level 3 outcome expectations	Level 4 outcome expectations
Pupils should be taught to:				
listen attentively to spoken language and show understanding by joining in and responding	Repeat words modelled by the teacher or on the audio enhanced e-storybooks and/or the audio file; listen and show understanding of single words	Listen and show understanding of short sentences/phrases said by the teacher or on the audio-enhanced e-storybooks and/or the audio file	Listen and show understanding of more complex sentences including conjunctions and a wider range of verbs	Listen and show understanding of short paragraphs containing familiar words and be able to work out the meaning of unfamiliar words shown in context
explore the patterns and sounds of language through songs and rhymes and link the spelling, sound and meaning of words	Repeat some words from the songs with accurate pronunciation; show understanding of single words	Sing and repeat phrases from the songs with accurate pronunciation and show understanding of their meaning; be able to spell single words from the songs	Pronounce familiar words and phrases correctly when singing songs and know their meaning; be able to find key words and phrases when looking at the song lyrics; be able to spell key words and phrases correctly	Be able to pronounce most words correctly when singing the songs and understand the lyrics; be able to reliably predict the pronunciation of unfamiliar words; be able to read and understand the song lyrics; be able to spell most words correctly
engage in conversations; ask and answer questions; express opinions and respond to those of others; seek clarification and help	Ask and answer simple questions regarding: their name, how old they are and how they are feeling	Ask and answer a wider range of questions such as when their birthday is using prompts. Give simple opinions about animals and hobbies	Be able to take part in simple conversations, reusing previously-seen vocabulary independently, talk about the weather and use a wider range of verbs	engage in conversations, using familiar questions and answers; express opinions using *aimer*, *detester* and *adorer* and ask others' opinions. Use *je voudrais* to ask for help
speak in sentences, using familiar vocabulary, phrases and basic language structures	Repeat sentences modelled by the teacher or those in the storybooks	Use familiar language within a given structure to create their own sentences and modify given sentences by changing one element	Use a limited number of high-frequency verbs and familiar language to say new sentences; use a given sentence starter to construct the rest of the sentence	Manipulate language to create and say own sentences using familiar language

National Curriculum programme of study	Level 1 outcome expectations	Level 2 outcome expectations	Level 3 outcome expectations	Level 4 outcome expectations
Pupils should be taught to:				
develop accurate pronunciation and intonation so that others understand when they are reading aloud or using familiar words and phrases	Pronounce most familiar words and phrases correctly, paying particular attention to sounds that are pronounced differently in French to English	Identify a range of sound-symbol correspondences in French and recognise them within vocabulary; speak with confidence	Pronounce familiar words and phrases correctly. Start to predict the pronunciation of unfamiliar words	Pronounce most words correctly. reliably predict the pronunciation of unfamiliar words in a sentence using knowledge of letter sounds and accents; talk clearly and with differentiated intonation for questions and statements.
present ideas and information to a range of audiences	Make simple statements about themselves	Give more detailed information about themselves and other people using a given structure	Give instructions to others and present simple descriptions of people and weather with more choice of vocabulary and structures	Present to others own ideas and information on familiar topics, using sentences with *parce que* to give a reason why
read carefully to show understanding of words, phrases and simple writing	Demonstrate understanding of key words and phrases through the role plays and by acting out mini-scripts, based on the storybooks	Demonstrate understanding of a wider range of vocabulary; read a range of words independently in context	Recognise previously-learned vocabulary in new contexts; show understanding of more complex sentences including conjunctions and adjectives in different forms.	Read and show understanding of the 28 storybooks and other short passages of text using familiar language; begin to infer meaning of unknown words in a given context, especially where words are cognates
appreciate stories, songs, poems and rhymes in the language	Understand and appreciate the main parts of the plot in the first 7 storybooks	Demonstrate a secure understanding of the storybooks at this level	Follow the text of the story books and be able to read out sections of the text	Read aloud the storybooks in this section; read and understand the gist of an unfamiliar text using familiar language
broaden their vocabulary and develop their ability to understand new words that are introduced into familiar written material, including through using a dictionary	Use context (illustrations/ cognates/ sentence structure) to predict the meaning of new words.	Learn a wider range of vocabulary, including verbs, nouns and adjectives; begin to use a bilingual dictionary with support to find extra words they want to express.	Recognise the imperative mood; recognise culturally-significant vocabulary to do with festivals and celebrations; use a bilingual dictionary independently to find new words	Build vocabulary as pupils progress through the storybooks; learn to gain the gist of texts and use a bilingual dictionary to find the meaning of words in written material and understand their meaning in context
write phrases from memory, and adapt these to create new sentences, to express ideas clearly	Write simple words from memory with understandable accuracy	Write short phrases from memory with increasing accuracy	Write simple sentences from memory, using familiar vocabulary	Write familiar complex sentences from memory, changing words to create new sentences with understandable accuracy

National Curriculum programme of study	Level 1 outcome expectations	Level 2 outcome expectations	Level 3 outcome expectations	Level 4 outcome expectations
Pupils should be taught to:				
Describe how they are feeling using simple language; introduce colours as adjectives that can be used to describe objects	Begin to use adjectives to describe pencil case items; recognise different forms of adjectives when describing a range of body part nouns	Use a range of vocabulary to write and say physical descriptions of people using the first person form of the verbs; manipulate adjective endings to agree with nouns;	Use a range of vocabulary to write and say physical descriptions of people using the first and third person form of the verbs; construct more complex sentences using conjunctions; manipulate familiar language to describe people, places, things and actions (using a bilingual dictionary when necessary)	Use a range of vocabulary to write and say physical descriptions of people using the first and third person form of the verbs; construct more complex sentences using conjunctions; manipulate familiar language to describe people, places, things and actions (using a bilingual dictionary when necessary)

National Curriculum programme of study	Level 1 outcome expectations	Level 2 outcome expectations	Level 3 outcome expectations	Level 4 outcome expectations
Pupils should be taught to:				
understand basic grammar appropriate to the language being studied, such as (where relevant): feminine, masculine and neuter forms and the conjugation of high-frequency verbs; key features and patterns of the language; how to apply these, for instance, to build sentences; and how these differ from or are similar to English	Know the 1st, 2nd and 3rd person singular pronouns; know the masculine and feminine definitive articles and use correctly; know that most adjectives appear after the noun; know how to make the plural form of some nouns; use the correct form of *avoir* in the present tense with 1st, 2nd and 3rd person pronouns; understand that possessive pronouns need to agree with the noun they are describing; construct simple sentences; know that apostrophes are used before words starting with a vowel to indicate elision	Understand that adjectives must agree with the noun they describe; know how to make the plural form of nouns (and that some plurals are irregular); use the correct form of *être* and some regular '*er*' verbs in the present tense with 1st, 2nd and 3rd pronouns; know that apostrophes are not used to show possession	Compare high-frequency verbs *avoir* and *être* in a range of contexts; recognise the imperative form of a range of regular verbs; begin to explore the structure of *je peux/je veux/tu veux* + infinitive; recognise and understand the conjugation of common regular and some irregular verbs in the present tense, including one reflexive verb, in certain persons; ensure that adjectives agree with the noun they are describing with some support	Demonstrate the use, in sentences, of the knowledge of grammar already learned: word classes, gender of nouns, definite and indefinite article, plural of nouns, 1st, 2nd and 3rd person pronouns with regular and high-frequency verbs in the present tense (including *avoir*, *être*, *aller*, *faire* and *pouvoir*), the position and agreement of adjectives; negatives; possessive pronouns (*mon, ma, mes, ton, ta, tes, son, sa, ses*); understanding and use of the immediate future tense (*aller* + infinitive); construct simple and some more complex sentences. Recognise the difference between regular and irregular verbs and how the pattern of conjugation changes. Understand the principle of reflexive verbs (e.g. *ils se disputent*). Recognise the use of the partitive article (*du, de la, de l', des*) and its relevance to the gender & number of nouns; recognise the use of *il faut* + infinitive. Notice the differences from and similarities to the English language

Bonjour

Unité 1

Exercice 1 – Écouter
Play the story (Audio Track 1), pausing as necessary. Ask the pupils if they understood any of the story. Could they hear any words that were the same as, or similar to, English words (cognates)?

Exercice 2 – Écouter/lire
Display the audio enhanced e-storybook on the IWB. Click on the speech bubbles to hear what the characters are saying. Ask the pupils if they understand more now. Brainstorm the meaning of the entire story as a class-wide exercise. To hear the pronunciation of individual words/phrases, click on the words in the *Vocabulaire* lists on each page or in the *Vocabulaire* list at the end of the book.

Exercice 3 – Écrire
Ask the pupils to look for cognates (words that are similar in English and French). Emphasise how the French word is pronounced differently to the English.

Ask pupils to write a French word in the air, or on a friend's back, which their friend must guess, for one point, and supply its meaning, for a further point. They can then do this in reverse, using the English word and asking for the French, but this only gains one point for the whole exercise! Model this exercise to the class first to ensure they understand what to do.

Vocabulaire
(Audio Track 2)
bonjour	good morning/hello
écoutez	listen
levez-vous	get up
regardez	look
un crocodile	a crocodile
non	no
c'est moi	it's me
maman	mum
alors	so
s'il vous plaît	please

Vocabulaire pour le professeur
(Audio Track 5)
Jaques a dit	Jack said (like Simon says)
maman dit	Mum says
silence	silence

Exercice 4 – Parler
Pupils act out the story (script of story is on *Feuille* 1a but it is best to do the exercise without it at this stage). For the first run-through, choose two of the more confident pupils to be Luc and Sophie and take the role of *maman* yourself. After this, choose another confident pupil to be *maman* with different pupils in the roles of Luc and Sophie. You could split the class up into smaller groups of three pupils, each acting out the story. Ensure all pupils act in at least one role.

Exercice 5 – Écouter/parler
Agree appropriate gestures to illustrate each of the commands:

Learn French with Luc et Sophie, Level 1
© Barbara Scanes and Brilliant Publications Limited

Play a game where:
- you say the command and the pupils have to make the appropriate gesture, and
- you make the gesture and the pupils must put up a hand to tell you the correct command.

Let a pupil take your place once the game has been played a few times and the pupils have understood what to do.

Exercice 6 – Écouter
Play *Jacques a dit* (Simon says). Model the game initially, using the commands from the story:

- *Levez-vous*
- *Écoutez*
- *Regardez*

> **Traduction de l'histoire**
>
> **Good morning**
> *page 2*
> Good morning Luc and Sophie!
> *page 3*
> Luc! Sophie! Listen!
> *page 4*
> Luc! Sophie! Get up!
> *page 5*
> Luc! Sophie! Look – a crocodile!
> *page 6*
> A crocodile?
> A crocodile!
> *page 7*
> No! It's me, Mum. Right, get up please!

Allow pupils to take the lead in this game once they are confident with the pronunciation.

Allow pupils to be back 'in' after two rounds to ensure continued participation.

Pupils love this game. It makes an excellent plenary for this unit and a fun game as an 'intermission' in any other. For variation, you could add in *s'il vous plaît* : *Jacques a dit levez-vous s'il vous plaît;* pupils can only move if you say please!

Exercice 7 – Chanter
Teach the song *Maman dit* to reinforce the vocabulary (*Feuille* 1b), Audio Tracks 3 and 4 (instrumental version).

Vocabulaire supplémentaire
Maman dit   Mum says
silence   silence

Feuille de travail
Feuilles de travail 1c and 1d reinforce the vocabulary learnt in the unit.

Grammaire

The imperative tense
In this unit we meet three examples of the imperative tense, which is used for commands and instructions:
- *Écoutez* – listen
- *Regardez* – look
- *Levez-vous* – get up/stand up

These are all plural/formal forms of commands and should, therefore, only be used for the whole class or more than one pupil. The exercises reflect this usage. The singular/informal forms are introduced in Level 3.

'You' in French
In French there are two forms of the word 'you'. *Vous* is the plural/formal word for 'you'. In **Learn French with Luc et Sophie, Level 1**, in order to avoid confusing pupils at this stage, it is only used in certain expressions, such as the commands above and those met in later units and also in the phrase *s'il vous plaît* (please).

Punctuation in French
As you will see from the song on page 19, the French use *guillemets* « », instead of inverted commas to show direct speech. In French a space is put after the opening *guillemet* and before the closing *guillemet*.

Bonjour

Maman: Bonjour, Luc et Sophie !

Luc! Sophie ! Écoutez !

Luc ! Sophie ! Levez-vous !

Luc ! Sophie! Regardez – un crocodile !

Luc: Un crocodile !

Sophie: Un crocodile ?

Maman: Non! C'est moi, maman.

Alors levez-vous s'il vous plaît !

Bonjour

Maman: Bonjour, Luc et Sophie !

Luc! Sophie ! Écoutez !

Luc ! Sophie ! Levez-vous !

Luc ! Sophie! Regardez – un crocodile !

Luc: Un crocodile !

Sophie: Un crocodile ?

Maman: Non! C'est moi, maman.

Alors levez-vous s'il vous plaît !

Maman dit

je m'appelle _____

Maman dit « Bonjour, Luc ! »
Silence, silence, silence.
Maman dit « Bonjour, Luc ! »
Silence, silence, silence.

Maman dit « Bonjour, Sophie ! »
Silence, silence, silence.
Maman dit « Bonjour, Sophie ! »
Silence, silence, silence.

Maman dit « Écoutez ! »
Silence, silence, silence.
Maman dit « Écoutez ! »
Silence, silence, silence.

Maman dit « Regardez
Le croco- crocodile »
Maman dit « Regardez
Le croco- crocodile ! »

Maman dit « C'est moi, c'est moi,
Et levez-vous alors ! »
Maman dit « C'est moi, c'est moi,
Et levez-vous alors ! »

Draw your own picture of maman, Luc and Sophie (and the crocodile, if you like!) in this box. Label the people you draw.

Regardez, un crocodile !

Draw lines to match up the French words with the correct pictures.

je m'appelle _____

bonjour

un crocodile

levez-vous

regardez

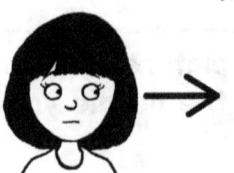

écoutez

maman

Bonjour Luc et Sophie !

1d
Feuille de travail

Colour in the picture and write what you think maman is saying in the speech bubble.

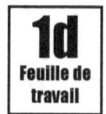

je m'appelle ________________

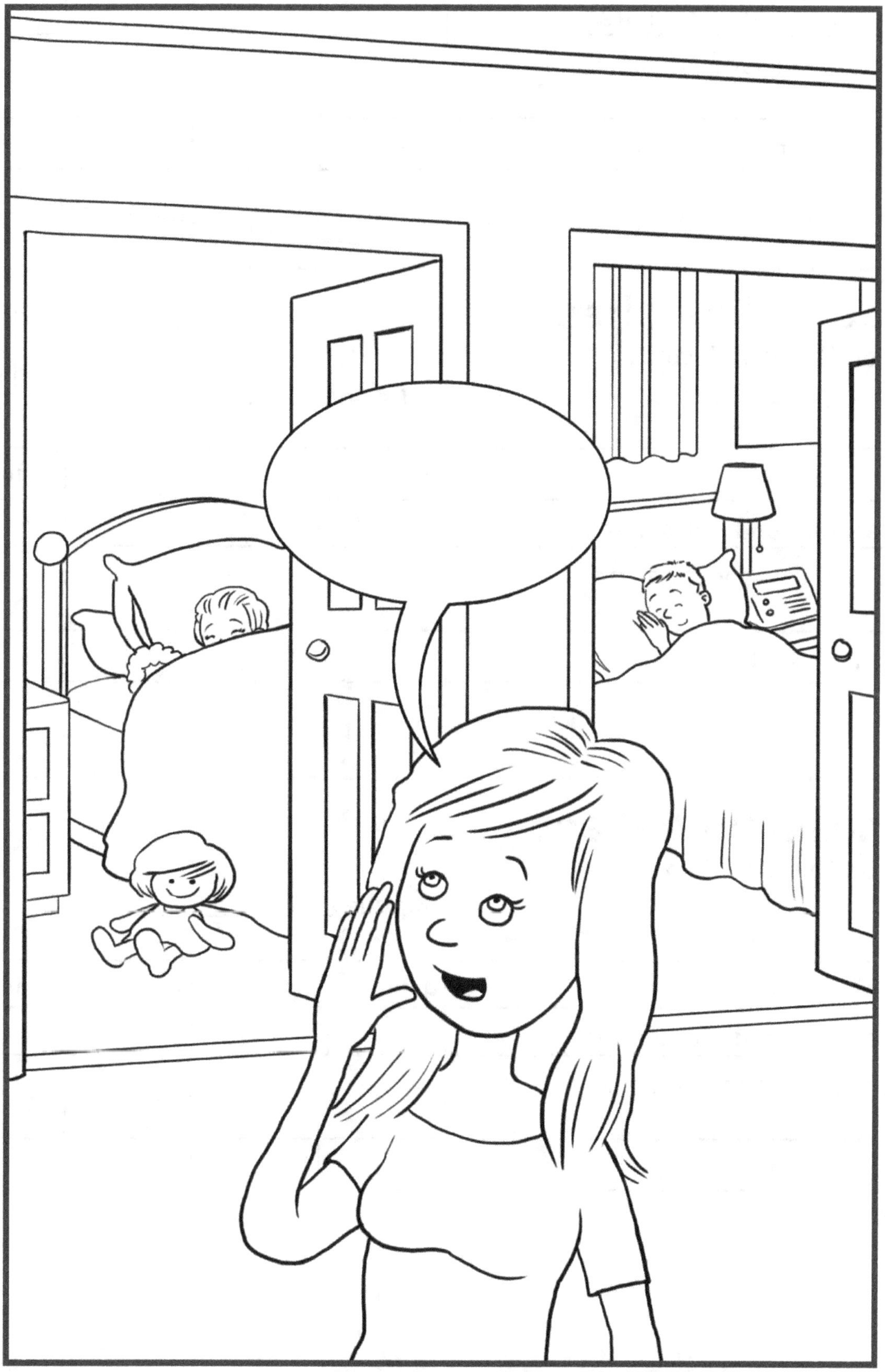

Self-assessment sheet
At the end of this unit I can...

Unité **1** Je peux...

je m'appelle _____

	date	not yet	nearly	definitely
greet my teacher and classmates				
understand and respond to some commands				
say 'please' in French				

- -

Self-assessment sheet
At the end of this unit I can...

Unité **1** Je peux...

je m'appelle _____

	date	not yet	nearly	definitely
greet my teacher and classmates				
understand and respond to some commands				
say 'please' in French				

- -

Self-assessment sheet
At the end of this unit I can...

Unité **1** Je peux...

je m'appelle _____

	date	not yet	nearly	definitely
greet my teacher and classmates				
understand and respond to some commands				
say 'please' in French				

Je m'appelle Sophie

Unité 2

Cinq minutes français
Start this, and every lesson henceforth, with around five minutes with only French spoken. Use gestures to help communicate and don't worry about using the occasional English word or phrase. When both you and your pupils are more familiar with the vocabulary, it will be easier and more natural for you to conduct the entire *Cinq minutes français* in French.

Greet the pupils with *bonjour* (good morning). Shake hands with a pupil and say *bonjour*. Demonstrate that they should shake hands with each other and say *bonjour*. Play *Jacques a dit* (see *Unité* 1, *Exercice* 6) using the commands learned in the previous unit.

Exercice 1 – Écouter
Play the story (Audio Track 6), pausing as necessary. Ask the pupils if they understood any of the story. Could they work out any of what was happening?

Exercice 2 – Écouter/lire

Display the audio enhanced e-storybook on the IWB. Click on the speech bubbles to hear what the characters are saying. Ask the pupils if they understand more now. Brainstorm the meaning of the entire story as a class-wide exercise. To hear the pronunciation of individual words/phrases, click on the words in the *Vocabulaire* lists on each page or in the *Vocabulaire* list at the end of the book.

Exercice 3 – Parler

Pupils act out the story (*Feuille* 2a). As teacher, assume a major role the first time around, eg that of Luc or Sophie, in order to give guidance to the pupils acting the other roles. After the first run-through, allocate all the roles to other pupils. Ask the non-acting pupils to listen out for pronunciation and, at the end of the scene, to comment positively on words that were pronounced correctly and offer positive criticism on those words which were not. As teacher, offer your own comment in the first instance, for example: 'Robert said *arrive*. Was that the right way to say that word in French?' Play Audio Track 6 again, stopping at the appropriate point, or listen to the vocabulary list (Audio Track 7), to check for the correct pronunciation.

Vocabulaire
(Audio Track 7)

ça va ?	how are you?/ are you OK?/ how are things?
ça va	I'm OK/things are OK
bien	well/fine
ça va bien	I'm very well
merci	thank you
comment t'appelles-tu ?	what's your name?
je m'appelle ...	my name is...
et toi ?	and you?
ça va mal	I'm not well/ things are bad
maman arrive	mum's coming
au revoir	goodbye

Vocabulaire déjà utilisé
bonjour	hello
non	no

Vocabulaire pour le professeur
(Audio Track 10)

cinq minutes français	5 minutes of French
tu sors du jeu	you're out (singular/ informal)

Je m'appelle Sophie   Unité 2

Exercice 4 – Écouter/parler
The object here is to practise the question *Ça va ?* and the three possible answers given in the story. First teach an action for the question *Ça va ?*, then the responses, one at a time.

Traduction de l'histoire

My name is Sophie
page 2
Hello, how are you doing?
Fine, thanks.
page 3
What's your name?
I'm called Mark. What about you? What's your name?
page 4
My name is Sophie. How are you doing?
Er… fine.
page 5
Hey! No, Sophie!
Ow! Mum!
page 6
Are you OK?
page 7
Oh no! That's really bad! Mum's coming. Bye!
Er… bye!

Model the game by asking the question *Ça va ?* with the appropriate gesture. Alter the order in which you say the response phrases and ask the pupils to supply the correct gesture to show they have understood. You could vary this game by making anyone who answers incorrectly 'out' for one turn or by turning it into a game of *Jacques a dit* (Simon says).

Next, ask a pupil to take your place as questioner and call out the different answers for his/her classmates to make the right gesture. Choose a different pupil to take the place of the questioner and continue with this game for a few turns then change the game so that the questioner makes the gesture and asks for the correct verbal answer to be supplied. This can become noisy but is good fun when carefully controlled and allowed to continue for just a couple of minutes.

Grammaire

Subject pronouns
In this unit we meet two personal pronouns:
❖ *je* – I
❖ *tu* – you

When writing *je* there is no need for a capital '*j*', unlike in English with 'I', unless the word occurs at the beginning of a sentence.

In this unit we meet the singular form of 'you', which is *tu*. It is also the informal form, ie that used for family, friends and animals. At this stage, there is no need to emphasise this point to pupils. It will become clear through usage when we meet the plural/formal form *vous* in later units. (Although we did meet *s'il vous plaît* and commands with *vous* in the previous unit.)

Finally, put the children into pairs and allow them to play the game between them, changing roles after a minute or two.

Exercice 5 – Parler
Practise asking and saying one's name by playing a 'chain' game. You, the teacher, start it by asking a pupil at the front or back: *Comment t'appelles-tu ?* That pupil must answer *je m'appelle ...* followed by his/her name and then turn to the next pupil and ask him or her *Comment t'appelles-tu ?* This question chain continues until the last pupil asks the first the same question and the chain has gone full circle.

After the first go-round, vary this exercise by timing how long it takes from the first pupil to the last and aiming to beat the record without skipping anybody or mispronouncing any of the words.

Finally, split the class into two halves and have them compete against each other to complete the chain quicker than the other half, again without skipping anybody or any mispronunciations.

Exercice 6 – Écouter/parler

Give each pupil one of the flashcards with a French name on it (page 32). These common French names have been chosen as they will help children learn to pronounce letter sounds that are different in French to English. Listen to Audio Track 11 for the correct pronunciation of each name. Next, play the track again and ask each child to pronounce their French name when they hear it; pause after each name to give pupils time to say, for example, *je m'appelle Hervé*. It can be funny to give the boys a girl's name and vice versa provided they are not sensitive about this.

Female names	**Male names**
Marie-France	Benoît
Mireille	Pascal
Élodie	Thierry
Yvette	Jean-Pierre
Anaïs	Didier
Anouk	Serge
Céline	Hervé

Have children swap their name cards with someone else. Again, they should listen out for their 'new' name on the audio file and repeat *je m'appelle...* and the name on the card.

Exercice 7 – Parler
Next, using the name cards again, ask the pupils to go around the class and ask as many of their classmates as they can in a given time: *Comment t'appelles-tu ?* To avoid 'cheating' in the form of rushing the question and not answering in full, impose the rule that no one needs to answer if the question is not asked properly and, similarly, a one-word answer (ie just the name) means they are 'out' (*Tu sors du jeu !*). This game is usually self-policing!

Play the game again. This time, children must find someone else with the same name as them. When they find that person, they both bring their cards to you and you give them each a new name from the stack of cards and the game starts again. Impose a time limit, eg 3–4 minutes.

Exercice 8 – Parler
Put children into groups to make up a role play using the vocabulary in the story. They must include:
- a greeting
- a farewell
- ask how someone is and give an answer
- ask and say one's name.

Exercice 9 – Écrire
Distribute pieces of card, folded in such a way that they will stand up by themselves on a desk, and ask each pupil to write, in big letters, *je m'appelle…*, with either their real English, or a fictitious French, name on it. They can decorate these with colours and stickers to put out on their desks at the start of every French lesson in future. It is important to check that they have spelt *je m'appelle…* correctly. Write it on the board and ask children to spell it out with you aloud. Encourage pupils to practise writing it in the air or on their sleeves before they attempt to write it on the card.

Exercice 10 – Chanter
Teach the song *Bonjour, ça va ?* to reinforce the vocabulary (*Feuille* 2b), Audio Tracks 8 and 9 (instrumental version).

Feuilles de travail
Feuilles de travail 2c, 2d and 2e reinforce the vocabulary learnt in the unit.

Je m'appelle Sophie

2a Petite pièce

Luc: Bonjour, ça va ?

Marc: Ça va bien, merci.

Luc: Comment t'appelles-tu ?

Marc: Je m'appelle Marc. Et toi ? Comment t'appelles-tu ?

Sophie: Je m'appelle Sophie ! Ça va ?

Marc: Euh ... ça va.

Luc: Eh ? Non, Sophie !

Sophie: Ouah ! Maman !

Marc: Ça va ?

Luc: Oh non ! Ça va mal. Maman arrive. Au revoir !

Marc: Euh ... au revoir !

Je m'appelle Sophie

2a Petite pièce

Luc: Bonjour, ça va ?

Marc: Ça va bien, merci.

Luc: Comment t'appelles-tu ?

Marc: Je m'appelle Marc. Et toi ? Comment t'appelles-tu ?

Sophie: Je m'appelle Sophie ! Ça va ?

Marc: Euh ... ça va.

Luc: Eh ? Non, Sophie !

Sophie: Ouah ! Maman !

Marc: Ça va ?

Luc: Oh non ! Ça va mal. Maman arrive. Au revoir !

Marc: Euh ... au revoir !

Bonjour, ça va ?

je m'appelle _____

2b Chanson

Bonjour, ça va ?
Comment t'appelles-tu ?
Je m'appelle Hervé
et ça va bien.

Bonjour, ça va ?
Comment t'appelles-tu ?
Je m'appelle Élodie
et oui, ça va.

Bonjour, ça va ?
Comment t'appelles-tu ?
Je m'appelle Serge
et ça va bien, merci.

Bonjour, ça va ?
Comment t'appelles-tu ?
Je m'appelle Mireille
et ça va mal !

Au revoir !

Draw a picture of you meeting a new friend. Write what you say in the speech bubbles.

Ça va bien, merci !

Fill in the speech bubbles to show what you think the children are saying.

je m'appelle _____

- Ça va ?
- Ça va
- Ça va bien
- Ça va mal

1.
2.
3.
4.

Ça va ?

Draw lines to match the correct pictures with the correct phrases.

je m'appelle _____

Ça va ?

Au revoir !

Je m'appelle Marc.

Comment t'appelles-tu ?

Bonjour ! Je m'appelle Sophie.

Luc et Marc

2e
Feuille de travail

Colour in the picture and write what you think Luc and Marc are saying in the speech bubbles.

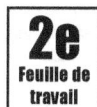

je m'appelle ______________________________

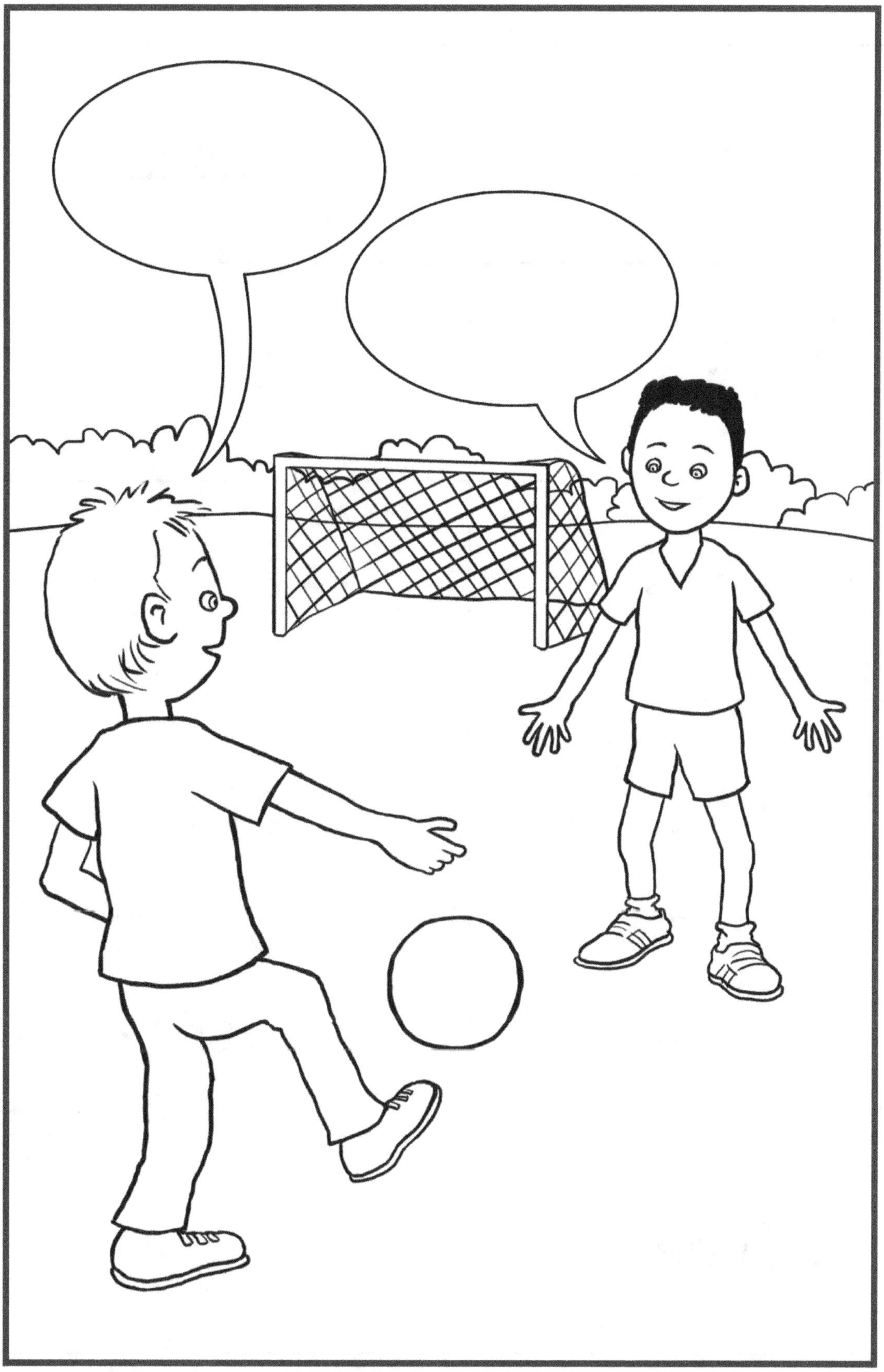

Marie-France	Benoît
Mireille	Pascal
Élodie	Thierry
Yvette	Jean-Pierre
Anaïs	Didier
Anouk	Serge
Céline	Hervé

Self-assessment sheet
At the end of this unit I can...

Unité 2 Je peux...

je m'appelle _____

	date	not yet	nearly	definitely
say goodbye to my teacher and classmates				
understand when asked my name				
say my name and ask somebody their name				
say how I'm feeling and ask someone else				

- -

Self-assessment sheet
At the end of this unit I can...

Unité 2 Je peux...

je m'appelle _____

	date	not yet	nearly	definitely
say goodbye to my teacher and classmates				
understand when asked my name				
say my name and ask somebody their name				
say how I'm feeling and ask someone else				

- -

Self-assessment sheet
At the end of this unit I can...

Unité 2 Je peux...

je m'appelle _____

	date	not yet	nearly	definitely
say goodbye to my teacher and classmates				
understand when asked my name				
say my name and ask somebody their name				
say how I'm feeling and ask someone else				

Combien de biscuits ?

Unité 3

Cinq minutes français

Greet the pupils with *Bonjour les enfants* (Good morning children) and elicit the reply: *Bonjour madame* or *Bonjour monsieur*. (Listen to Audio Track 18 for the correct pronunciation of these words and practise them with the children.) Ask the class: *ça va ?* and elicit the general reply: *ça va bien, merci*. You can then ask a few individual children *ça va ?* Ask one child to ask another or do this as a question chain around the whole class. Practise asking and answering the question: *comment t'appelles-tu ?* around the room, encouraging individual pupils to ask their classmates. Alternatively, set up role plays in pairs with children greeting, asking *ça va ?* and answering, asking and answering *comment t'appelles-tu ?* and finishing with *au revoir*.

At the end of the lesson, say *Au revoir, les enfants* and elicit the reply, *Au revoir, madame* or *Au revoir, monsieur*.

Exercice 1 – Écouter

Play the story (Audio Track 12), pausing as necessary. Ask the pupils if they understood any of the story. Could they work out any of what was happening?

Exercice 2 – Écouter/lire

Display the audio enhanced e-storybook on the IWB. Click on the speech bubbles to hear what the characters are saying. Ask the pupils if they understand more now. Brainstorm the meaning of the entire story as a class-wide exercise. To hear the pronunciation of individual words/phrases, click on the words in the *Vocabulaire* lists on each page or in the *Vocabulaire* list at the end of the book.

Exercice 3 – Chanter

Teach the song *Un biscuit, deux biscuits* to reinforce the vocabulary (*Feuille* 3b), Audio Tracks 14 and 15 (instrumental version).

Exercice 4 – Chanter

Ask the pupils to show you two hands. Count fingers as you sing along with Audio Tracks 16 and 17 (instrumental version).

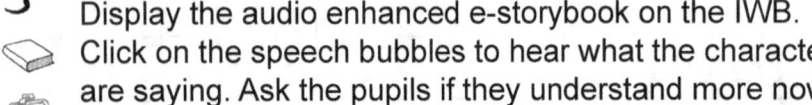

Un, deux, trois, quatre, cinq, six, sept, huit, neuf et dix

Vocabulaire
(Audio Track 13)

combien de biscuits ?	how many biscuits?
j'ai	I have
tu as	you have
un biscuit	a biscuit
des biscuits	some biscuits
salut	hi (or bye)
oui	yes
ils sont	they are
pour	for
mes poupées	my dolls
mais	but
beaucoup (de)	lots (of)
un	one
deux	two
trois	three
quatre	four
cinq	five
six	six
sept	seven
huit	eight
neuf	nine
dix	ten
combien (de) ?	how much/many of?
moi	me

Vocabulaire déjà utilisé

bonjour	hello
ça va ?	how are you?
regardez	look
non	no

Vocabulaire pour le professeur (Audio Track 18)	
les enfants	(the) children
madame	Mrs/'Miss'
monsieur	Mr/'Sir' (at school)

This is *La chanson des numéros* (the number song) that will be referred to in future units.

Exercice 5 – Parler/écouter
Divide the pupils into four groups, giving each group a pack of numeral flashcards (page 43). One pupil takes a card at random, looks at it and then hides it behind his/her back. The other pupils must then try to guess the correct number on the flashcard asking, for example, *Tu as le numéro cinq ?* The pupil hiding the card must answer either *non* or, if the guess is correct, *oui, j'ai le numéro cinq*. Another pupil then takes a turn at taking and hiding a card until all the pupils have had a go.

Another variation on this game is for the pupil who makes the correct guess to 'win' the card and the game is over when the cards are all gone. Obviously, with this variation, there is a process of elimination. However, this does not detract from the aim of the game, namely to learn the French names for the numbers.

Traduction de l'histoire

How many biscuits?
page 2
Hello Chloé. Hello Martine.
Hello, Lucie. How are you?
Look, I've got some biscuits.
page 3
Hi Sophie! Oh biscuits!
Yes, they're for my dolls.
page 4
Oh, but you've got lots of biscuits!
Yes! 1, 2, 3, 4, 5, 6, 7, 8, 9, 10.
page 5
And how many dolls do you have?
1, 2, 3, 4, 5, 6, 7, 8, 9.
page 6
You have 10 biscuits but only 9 dolls, so you've got a biscuit for me!
page 7
No, Luc! Mum!

Exercice 6 – Écouter
Pupils listen to the numbers spoken out of sequence on Audio Track 19. Pause the track after each number and ask children to show you the correct number of fingers.

deux
cinq
dix
sept
quatre
six
huit
neuf
un
trois

Exercice 7 – Parler
Distribute number flashcards (page 44) at random to ten pupils. Firstly, the pupils must arrange themselves in the correct number order.

Secondly, they must say which number they are holding, for example: *j'ai le numéro huit*. The remaining pupils must watch closely to see who is holding which number. Next, the pupils with the flashcards must hide them behind their backs and then rearrange themselves into a different order. The remaining pupils then have the chance to win a card/take a child's place by asking: *Tu as le numéro six ?* to which the corresponding pupil must answer *non* or *oui, j'ai le numéro six* as appropriate.

Another variation of this game is for the pupils with the flashcards to swap the number cards among themselves. This makes it harder for the remaining pupils to guess and the game should be allowed to continue for a shorter period and then the entire line-up of pupils is changed in order to give everyone a chance.

Exercice 8 – Écrire
An easy 'air writing' game is to put pupils into teams or pairs and ask one pupil to write a number in the air, or on another pupil's back. The correct guess gains a point and the turn passes to the other pupil.

Exercice 9 – Écrire
Pupils make a poster with the title *Les numéros* to illustrate the numbers in French from 1–10. Allow them to draw the digits in different colours, styles, fonts etc (as long as they are clear and legible) and then label them with the correct French number word. They could even draw the correct number of an object, eg 10 cars, and then write the word *dix* underneath the drawing. Check their spelling carefully.

Feuilles de travail
Feuilles de travail 3c, 3d and 3e reinforce the vocabulary learnt in the unit.

Grammaire

Note: this grammar section is intended to provide background for non-specialist teachers and is not intended to be taught formally to pupils. Pupils will learn the appropriate grammar through usage in the context of the stories and exercises.

Avoir (to have)
In this story we meet two forms of the verb *avoir*:

j'ai	I have
tu as	you have

If you add a question mark at the end (*tu as ?*) and a rising intonation, it means 'have you?' or 'have you got?' You may also see the words the other way round (*as-tu ?*).

Être (to be)
The third person plural present tense of *être* is also introduced in this unit:

sont	are
ils sont	they are (used for two or more males or a mixture of males* and females*)
elles sont	they are (used only for two or more females*)

*Note: as all nouns in French are also masculine or feminine, the subject pronouns *ils* and *elles* are used for **things** as well as people.

My
There are three ways of saying 'my' in French. This is explained in greater detail in *Unité 5*:

ma	feminine singular	ma poupée	my doll
mon	masculine singular	mon biscuit	my biscuit
mes	plural (masculine and feminine)	mes poupées	my dolls
		mes biscuits	my biscuits

The
Please note: *les poupées* means 'the dolls'. There are four French words for 'the':

le	masculine singular	le biscuit	the biscuit
la	feminine singular	la poupée	the doll
l'	used for both masculine and feminine singular before a noun beginning with a vowel or 'h'	l'homme l'an	the man the year
les	plural (masculine and feminine)	les poupées	the dolls

There are more examples of this grammatical point in Level 2.

Numbers
The pronunciation of '*six*' and '*dix*' changes when they come before a noun, for example: '*six biscuits*' is pronounced '*see bees-kwee*' and '*dix biscuits*' is pronounced '*dee bees-kwee*'.

Combien de biscuits ?

Sophie: Bonjour, Chloé. Bonjour Martine.

Bonjour Lucie. Ça va ?

Regardez, j'ai des biscuits.

Luc: Salut Sophie ! Oh ! Des biscuits !

Sophie: Oui, ils sont pour mes poupées.

Luc: Oh, mais tu as beaucoup de biscuits !

Sophie: Oui! Un, deux, trois, quatre, cinq, six, sept, huit, neuf, dix.

Luc: Et tu as combien de poupées ?

Sophie: Un, deux, trois, quatre, cinq, six, sept, huit, neuf.

Luc: Alors, tu as **dix** biscuits mais tu as **neuf** poupées.

Alors, tu as un biscuit pour moi !

Sophie: Non, Luc ! Ouah! Maman !

Un biscuit, deux biscuits

je m'appelle _____

3b Chanson

Un biscuit, deux biscuits, trois biscuits pour toi.

 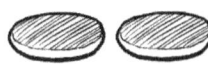 

Quatre biscuits, cinq biscuits, six biscuits pour moi.

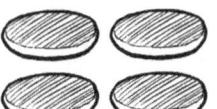 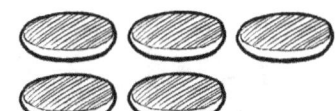 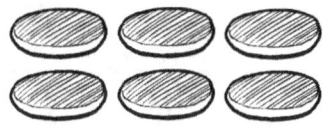

Sept biscuits, huit biscuits pour mes neuf poupées.

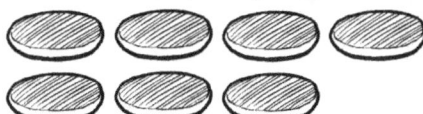 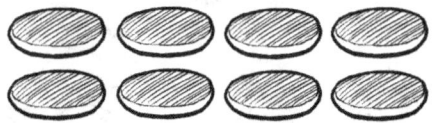

Dix biscuits ? Dix biscuits ! Ah oui – regardez !

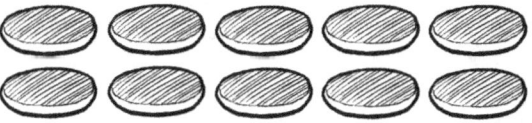

Combien ?

Count the objects in French and write the correct French number word next to the picture.

je m'appelle _____

Par exemple:

   trois
_____

1.    _____

2.    _____

3.    _____

4.    _____

5.    _____

6.    _____

7.

8.    _____

Combien ?

Draw a line between the French word and the correct number.

3d
Feuille de travail

je m'appelle ____________________________

1

2

3

4

5

6

7

8

9

10

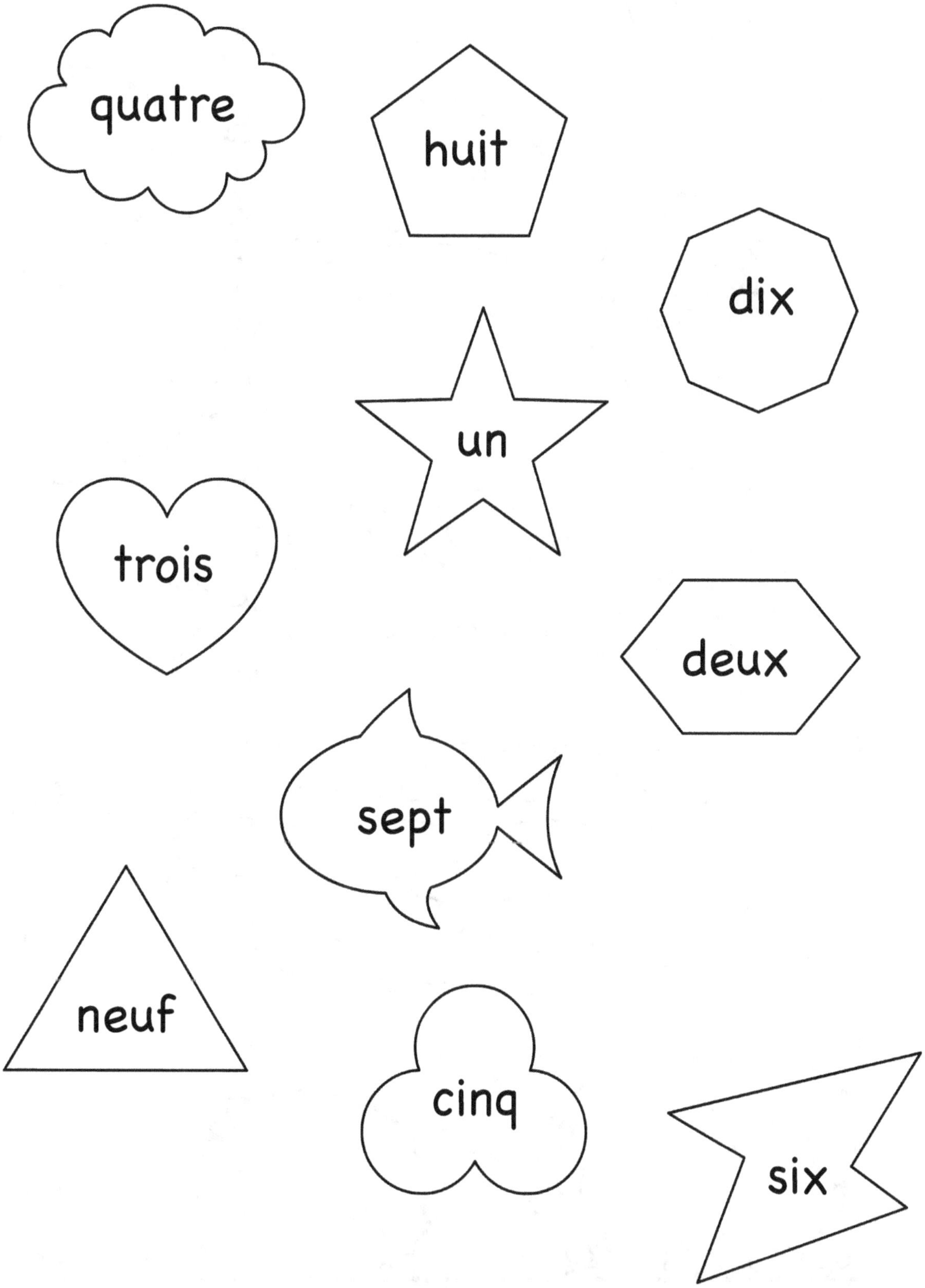
quatre
huit
dix
un
trois
deux
sept
neuf
cinq
six

Combien de biscuits ?

Colour in the picture and write what you think Sophie is saying in the speech bubble.

je m'appelle _____

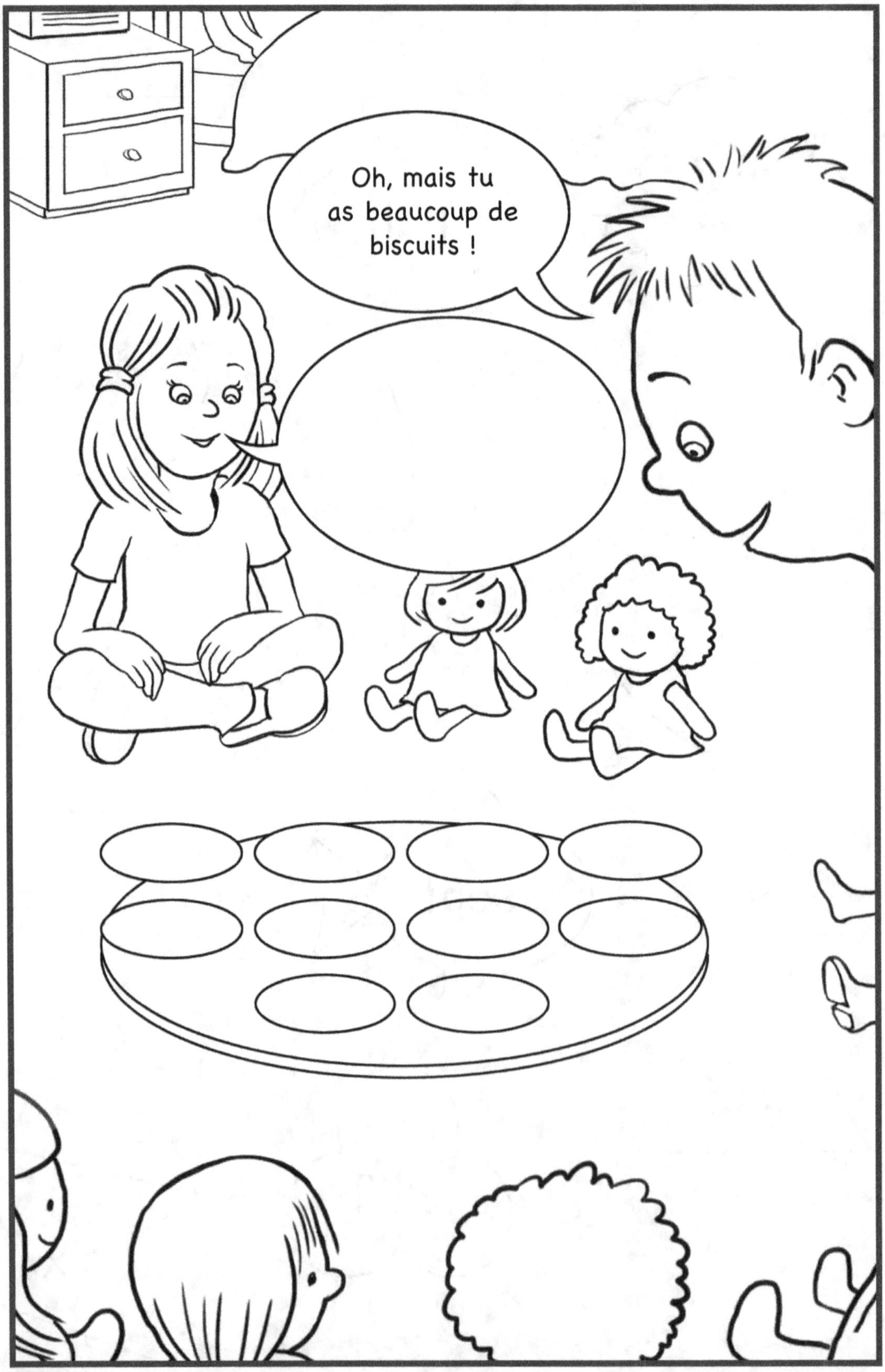

> Oh, mais tu as beaucoup de biscuits !

Combien de biscuits ? — Unité 3

1	2
3	4
5	6
7	8
9	10

un	deux
trois	quatre
cinq	six
sept	huit
neuf	dix

Self-assessment sheet
At the end of this unit I can...

Unité 3 Je peux...

je m'appelle _____

	date	not yet	nearly	definitely
recognise numbers to ten				
count to ten				
say the word 'biscuit' in the French way				

- -

Self-assessment sheet
At the end of this unit I can...

Unité 3 Je peux...

je m'appelle _____

	date	not yet	nearly	definitely
recognise numbers to ten				
count to ten				
say the word 'biscuit' in the French way				

- -

Self-assessment sheet
At the end of this unit I can...

Unité 3 Je peux...

je m'appelle _____

	date	not yet	nearly	definitely
recognise numbers to ten				
count to ten				
say the word 'biscuit' in the French way				

J'ai six ans

Unité 4

5 Cinq minutes français

Start the lesson with *Cinq minutes français*. Greet the pupils with *bonjour les enfants* eliciting *bonjour madame/monsieur* in reply. Ask: *Ça va ?* and elicit: *ça va bien, merci*. Practise counting to 10 in French, firstly as a group, then in sequence, pointing to one pupil after another in order. *Maintenant comptez en français !* (Now count in French!) Finally, count in sequence pointing to pupils at random. You could repeat one of the previous *Cinq minutes français* exercises, practising *Ça va ?* or *Comment t'appelles-tu ?*

At the end of each lesson, say *au revoir, les enfants* and elicit the reply, *au revoir, madame/monsieur*.

Exercice 1 – Écouter

Play the story (Audio Track 20), pausing as necessary. Ask the pupils if they understood any of the story. Could they work out any of what was happening?

Exercice 2 – Écouter/lire

Display the audio enhanced e-storybook on the IWB. Click on the speech bubbles to hear what the characters are saying. Ask the pupils if they understand more now. Brainstorm the meaning of the entire story as a class-wide exercise. To hear the pronunciation of individual words/phrases, click on the words in the *Vocabulaire* lists on each page or in the *Vocabulaire* list at the end of the book.

Exercice 3 – Parler

Firstly, practise the pronunciation of *Quel âge as-tu ?* and the answer (*j'ai … ans*). Initiate a question chain with you, the teacher, starting by asking a first pupil *Quel âge as-tu ?* and eliciting the answer: eg *j'ai sept ans*. The first pupil asks the next and so on until the chain is complete when the last pupil asks the first and that pupil answers with his/her age.

Exercice 4 – Parler

Choose three pupils to act out the play (*Feuille* 4a). If appropriate, ask another three to perform it again.

Next, divide the class into groups and ask them to make up their own role play using the vocabulary on the flashcards (page 53). The role plays should include:

Vocabulaire
(Audio Track 21)

quel âge as-tu ?	how old are you?
j'ai six ans	I'm six (years old)
tu as sept ans	you're seven (years old)
tu as sept ans ?	Are you seven (years old)?
c'est	it is
bientôt	soon
mon anniversaire	my birthday
en ce moment	at the moment
tu es	you are
un bébé	a baby

Vocabulaire déjà utilisé

bonjour	hello
comment t'appelles-tu ?	what's your name?
et toi ?	and you?
j'ai	I have
je m'appelle …	my name is…
mais	but
non	no
oui	yes

Vocabulaire pour le professeur
(Audio Track 24)

maintenant, comptez en français !	now count in French!
onze	eleven

- giving a greeting
- asking and saying how one is
- asking and saying one's name
- asking and saying one's age
- saying goodbye

The pupils can give made-up names and ages if they wish.

Vocabulaire pour le professeur (cont)	
j'aurai	I will be (have)*
peut-être	maybe
tu en auras	you will be (have)*
comme	like
un éléphant	an elephant

*See *Grammaire* box.

Exercice 5 – Écouter/parler

Listen to Audio Tracks 25 and/or 26 of a French speaker pronouncing the various ages. Pause the track and ask pupils to show the appropriate number of fingers for the age stated and to repeat the pronunciation after the speaker. The numbers are given in order on Track 25 and randomly on Track 26.

Audio Track 25	**Audio Track 26**
j'ai un an	*j'ai six ans*
j'ai deux ans	*j'ai un an*
j'ai trois ans	*j'ai huit ans*
j'ai quatre ans	*j'ai dix ans*
j'ai cinq ans	*j'ai trois ans*
j'ai six ans	*j'ai deux ans*
j'ai sept ans	*j'ai neuf ans*
j'ai huit ans	*j'ai quatre ans*
j'ai neuf ans	*j'ai sept ans*
j'ai dix ans	*j'ai cinq ans*

Traduction de l'histoire

I'm six
page 2
Hello, my name is Sophie.
What's your name?
My name is Nadine. How old are you?
page 3
I'm six. And you?
I'm five.
page 4
I'm eight.
page 5
No, you're seven!
It will soon be my birthday.
page 6
Yes, but you're seven at the moment!
And you, you're a baby!
page 7
No!
Ow! Mum!

Exercice 6 – Écouter/parler

Put pupils into pairs and give each pair a set of number flashcards (page 44). Pupil A asks Pupil B *quel âge as-tu ?* and holds up a flashcard at random. Pupil B must answer, eg *j'ai ... an(s)*, depending on the number shown on the flashcard. After a few turns, the pupils swap over.

Exercice 7 – Chanter

Ask the pupils to listen to the rap *Quel âge as-tu ?* on Audio Tracks 22 and 23 (instrumental version). Play it all the way through once, with the pupils just listening. On the second playing, pause the track after each line and ask the pupils to indicate the age that they have heard by showing the appropriate number of fingers, eg *j'ai cinq ans* requires the showing of five fingers. After a brief visual check of the show of fingers, say the correct number in French and ask the pupils to tell you what that number is in English and see if they were right. You can play the song a third time to give the children another opportunity to show they have understood the numbers/ages correctly. Finally, show the lyrics on the whiteboard (*Feuille* 4b) and encourage the children to sing along.

Vocabulaire supplémentaire

onze	eleven
j'aurai	I will be (literally: I will have*)
peut-être	maybe
tu en auras cent	you will be 100 (literally: you will have*)
comme	like
un éléphant	an elephant

*See *Grammaire* box

Feuille de travail
Feuilles de travail 4c and 4d reinforce the vocabulary learnt in the unit.

Grammaire

Talking about ages in French
J'ai means 'I have' (or 'I've got'). *Tu as* means 'you have' (or 'you've got') and, with the words the other way round (*As-tu ?*) means 'Have you?' (or 'Have you got?'). Very often, to ask a question in French, you simply add a question mark when writing, or just raise the inflection of your voice, to indicate a question, when speaking.

eg   *Tu as cinq ans.*
      Tu as cinq ans ?

In French, you say I **have** seven years and you ask, 'What age **have** you (got)?' This sounds strange in English but it is perfectly normal in French!

You also use *j'ai* and *tu as* (or *As-tu ?*) when talking about things (or people!) you have, for example, *j'ai un poney* (I have a pony/I've got a pony), *tu as un papa* (you have a Dad/you've got a Dad).

Tu en auras 100
In the song the phrase *tu en auras 100* is used. As explained above, in French you use the verb *avoir*, when talking about one's age, hence the use of *j'aurai* (I will have) and *tu auras* (you will have) in the song. The word *en* means 'in' but also 'of it/of them'. In the context of the song, *tu en auras 100* means 'you will have 100 **of them** (ie 100 years)'.

J'ai six ans

Sophie: Bonjour, je m'appelle Sophie. Comment t'appelles-tu ?

Nadine: Je m'appelle Nadine. Quel âge as-tu ?

Sophie: J'ai six ans. Et toi ?

Nadine: J'ai cinq ans.

Luc: Moi, j'ai huit ans.

Sophie: Non, tu as sept ans !

Luc: C'est bientôt mon anniversaire.

Sophie: Oui, mais tu as sept ans en ce moment !

Luc: Et toi, tu es un bébé.

Sophie: Non !

Luc: Ouah! Maman !

- -

J'ai six ans

Sophie: Bonjour, je m'appelle Sophie. Comment t'appelles-tu ?

Nadine: Je m'appelle Nadine. Quel âge as-tu ?

Sophie: J'ai six ans. Et toi ?

Nadine: J'ai cinq ans.

Luc: Moi, j'ai huit ans.

Sophie: Non, tu as sept ans !

Luc: C'est bientôt mon anniversaire.

Sophie: Oui, mais tu as sept ans en ce moment !

Luc: Et toi, tu es un bébé.

Sophie: Non !

Luc: Ouah! Maman !

Quel âge as-tu ?

je m'appelle

_____

Quel âge as-tu ? J'ai cinq ans.

Non, tu as quatre ans !

Quel âge as-tu ? J'ai six ans.

Oui, tu as six ans !

    Quel âge as-tu ? J'ai sept ans.

    Non, tu as six ans !

    Quel âge as-tu ? J'ai huit ans.

    Oui, tu as huit ans !

Quel âge as-tu ? J'ai neuf ans.

Non, tu as sept ans !

Quel âge as-tu ? J'ai dix ans.

Oui, tu as dix ans !

    Quel âge as-tu ? J'ai onze ans.

    Non, tu as dix ans !

    C'est bientôt mon anniversaire

    et j'aurai onze ans !

    Ou peut-être tu en auras

    cent comme un éléphant !

Draw the correct number of candles on each cake.

Quel âge as-tu ?

Fill in the gaps in the speech bubbles with the correct number from the box at the bottom of the page.

je m'appelle _____

1. J'ai _____ ans. — Sophie

2. J'ai _____ ans. — Nadine

3. J'ai _____ ans. — Luc

4. J'ai ___9___ ans.

5. J'ai ___3___ ans.

| un | deux | trois | quatre | cinq |
| six | sept | huit | neuf | dix |

Learn French with Luc et Sophie, Level 1
© Barbara Scanes and Brilliant Publications Limited

Quel âge as-tu ?

4d
Feuille de travail

Colour in the picture and write what you think Sophie and Nadine are saying in the speech bubbles.

je m'appelle ___________________________

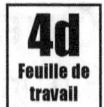

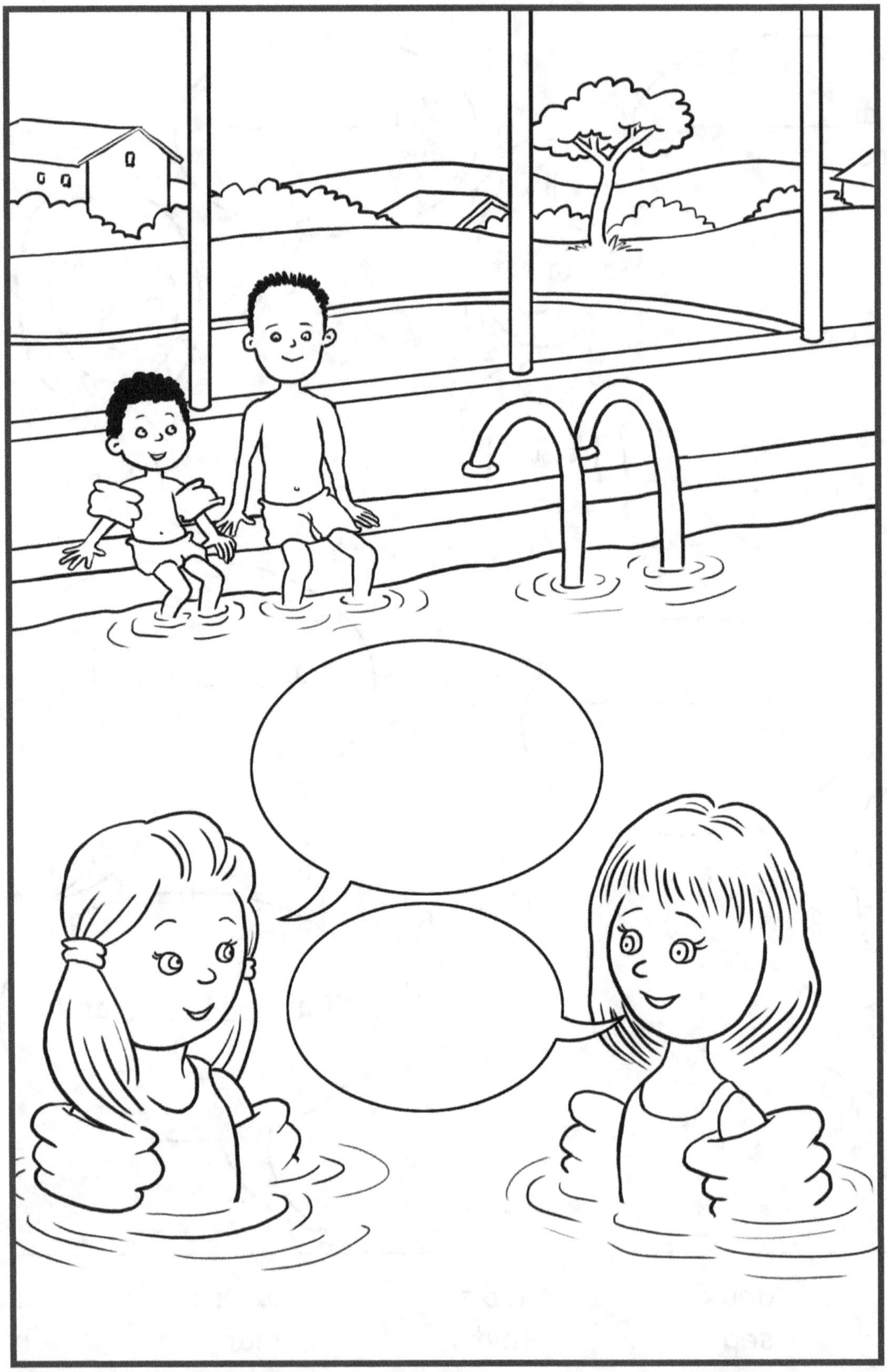

Bonjour	J'ai cinq ans
Et toi ?	Non !
Maman !	Je m'appelle Sophie.
Comment t'appelles-tu ?	Tu es un bébé.
Tu as sept ans.	Je m'appelle Nadine.
J'ai huit ans.	Quel âge as-tu ?
Oui.	C'est bientôt mon anniversaire.

Self-assessment sheet
At the end of this unit I can...

Unité **4** Je peux...

je m'appelle _____

	date	not yet	nearly	definitely
understand when somebody asks me my age				
say how old I am				
ask someone else how old they are				

- -

Self-assessment sheet
At the end of this unit I can...

Unité **4** Je peux...

je m'appelle _____

	date	not yet	nearly	definitely
understand when somebody asks me my age				
say how old I am				
ask someone else how old they are				

- -

Self-assessment sheet
At the end of this unit I can...

Unité **4** Je peux...

je m'appelle _____

	date	not yet	nearly	definitely
understand when somebody asks me my age				
say how old I am				
ask someone else how old they are				

J'ai un frère

Unité 5

 ## Cinq minutes français

Begin the lesson, as before, with greetings in French, asking *Ça va ?* and eliciting responses.

Recap the previous lesson(s) with short games to practise asking *Quel âge as-tu ?*, asking quick-fire questions at random to pupils.

Revise numbers 1–10 with *La chanson des numéros* (the number song) (Audio Tracks 16 and 17). Introduce the activity by saying: *Alors, maintenant chantez !* (Now sing!)

 ## Exercice 1 – Écouter

Play the story (Audio Track 27), pausing as necessary. Ask the pupils if they understood any of the story. Could they work out any of what was happening?

 ## Exercice 2 – Écouter/lire

Display the audio enhanced e-storybook on the IWB. Click on the speech bubbles to hear what the characters are saying. Ask the pupils if they understand more now. Brainstorm the meaning of the entire story as a class-wide exercise. To hear the pronunciation of individual words/phrases, click on the words in the *Vocabulaire* lists on each page or in the *Vocabulaire* list at the end of the book.

 ## Exercice 3 – Parler

Choose three pupils to play the roles of Sophie, Luc and Nadine and act out the story using the script (*Feuille* 5a) as a prompt. Again, ask the remaining pupils for positive feedback on their pronunciation. Now, either choose three more pupils to act out the story or make it a class-wide activity in groups of three. If there is an odd number, ask the 'odd' pupils to choose a name and engage in the role play, using the vocabulary they have learnt, to ask and say their names and ages. This is a useful extension exercise for the more able pupils.

 ## Exercice 4 - Écouter

Listen to Audio Track 32. Ask the children to listen carefully and put their hands up when they think they know how many brothers and sisters – if any – are being talked about.

Vocabulaire
(Audio Track 28)

tu as ?	have you (got)?
des frères	some brothers
des sœurs	some sisters
ou	or
une sœur	a sister
une petite sœur	a little sister
un frère	a brother
deux frères	two brothers
elle a trois ans	she is three years old
je voudrais	I would like
c'est qui ?	who is that?/ who is it?
mon frère	my brother
il est	he is
bête	silly
être	to be
enfant unique	only child

Vocabulaire déjà utilisé

c'est	it is
deux	two
et toi ?	and you?
j'ai	I have
mais	but
oui	yes
salut	hi

j'ai un frère
j'ai une sœur
j'ai deux frères
j'ai deux sœurs
j'ai un frère et une sœur
j'ai un frère et deux sœurs
j'ai deux frères et une sœur
j'ai deux frères et deux sœurs
je suis enfant unique

Vocabulaire pour le professeur	
(Audio Track 31)	
alors, maintenant chantez !	now sing!
un père	a father
une mère	a mother
un beau-père	a step father
une belle-mère	a step mother
un demi-frère	a half brother/ step brother
une demi-sœur	a half sister/ step sister
voici	here (is)
ma famille	my family
ma grande famille	my big family
je suis	I am

Exercice 5 – Parler

Ask the class the question: *Tu as des frères ou des sœurs ?* Check they understand/remember what the question means. Model some answers using the whiteboard and Audio Track 32.

Highlight the difference between *j'ai **un** frère* and *j'ai **une** sœur*. Explain that *un* – meaning one or 'a' – is for a boy and *une* for a girl. Practise the pronunciation of these words. A fun way to practise the unique *'u'* sound in French, is to tell the children to make their lips into the shape they need to make the sound 'oo' but then say 'ee' instead. It will sound strange and take practice but it works!

Point out, too, that the plural forms of these words take a final 's', just as in English, but that the 's' is not pronounced (there are exceptions to this rule which will be met later).

Ask pupils at random whether they have brothers and sisters. Encourage them to answer using one of the modelled answers. For other combinations of siblings, change the numbers accordingly.

Exercice 6 – Parler

Now put pupils into groups according to the number of siblings they have. For example, there will be a group of only children (*je suis enfant unique*), a group of one brother (*j'ai un frère*) etc.

Ask the first group, for example *je suis enfant unique* to move to another group and ask: *Tu as des frères ou des sœurs ?* The other group answers in unison, for example, *j'ai un frère*. Then it is that group's turn to ask a different group the question.

Finally, ask children to count, in French, how many are in each group.

Exercice 7 – Parler/écouter

Introduce two new words: *un père* (father) and *une mère* (mother) (modelled on Audio Track 31). Ask the children if they can tell you which of the 'my' words (*mon/ma/mes*) is the correct one to use with these words.

Choose two pupils at random to start with and ask them to pretend they are siblings. Ask the remaining pupils to ask them the question: *C'est qui ?* (who's that?) The two pupils must introduce each other to the class saying, for example, *c'est mon frère* or *c'est ma sœur*.

J'ai un frère — Unité 5

Choose different pupils to model this to the class.

Next, put pupils into pairs and give them 30 seconds to go around other pairs asking *C'est qui ?* and answering *c'est mon frère* or *c'est ma sœur*. After 30 seconds get pupils to swap partners and go again.

To expand this activity, ask pupils to pretend that they are each other's mother or father and introduce each other as *c'est mon père* or *c'est ma mère*. Pupils generally find this amusing!

As a further extension exercise, you can ask the pupils to say how many siblings they would like, eg *je voudrais un frère* or even, as Sophie says, *je voudrais être enfant unique !*

> **Traduction de l'histoire**
>
> **I have a brother**
> *page 2*
> Do you have any brothers or sisters, Nadine?
> *page 3*
> Yes, I have two brothers and a little sister. She is three. What about you?
> *page 4*
> I have a brother, but I would like a sister.
> *page 5*
> Hi!
> *page 6*
> Oh! Who's that?
> *page 7*
> It's my brother. He's silly. Oh, I wish I were an only child!

Exercice 8 – Écrire

Ask the pupils to make a poster about their family with the title '*Ma famille*' (my family). Ask the pupils if they can tell you what this means and, also, why the 'my' word used here is *ma* (because *famille* is feminine).

Pupils may draw stick people if they really don't enjoy drawing. Label each person in the poster as appropriate. For parents, use the labels *mon père* and *ma mère*. For siblings, label them as *mon frère* and *ma sœur*. If they wish to, the pupils may label with the person's name as well, eg *mon frère, Peter* or *ma sœur, Lucy*. Ask them to include themselves in the poster, labelling themselves *moi* (me) and adding *je m'appelle ….*

Check spellings carefully, especially accents. *Sœur* is often misspelt, so ask your pupils to make up mnemonics to help them remember, eg 'sisters often eat ugly raisins', and let pupils choose the best one.

If necessary, introduce the following vocabulary (modelled on Audio Track 31):

Vocabulaire supplémentaire

un beau-père	step father
une belle-mère	step mother
un demi-frère	a half brother/step brother
une demi-sœur	a half sister/step sister

Exercice 9 – Chanter

Teach the song *Voici ma famille* to reinforce the vocabulary (*Feuille* 5b), Audio Tracks 29 and 30 (instrumental version).

Vocabulaire supplémentaire

voici	here (is)
ma famille	my family
ma grande famille	my big family

J'ai un frère Unité 5

Feuilles de travail
Feuilles de travail 5c, 5d and 5e reinforce the vocabulary learnt in the unit.

 # Grammaire

Possessive pronouns
Explain to the pupils that, in French, there are three words for 'my'. We have already met one French word for 'my' in the previous unit (*mes poupées*). In this unit's story we meet another French word for 'my': *mon*, as in *mon frère*. Now introduce the feminine word for 'my': *ma*, as in *ma sœur* (my sister) or *ma mère* (my mother).

Remind your pupils that even **things** in French are masculine or feminine.

Practise the different French words for 'my':

ma	used when the person or thing belonging to you is feminine, for example, *ma sœur* (my sister); *ma poupée* (my doll)
mon	used when the person or thing belonging to you is masculine, for example, *mon frère* (my brother); *mon biscuit* (my biscuit)
mes	plural word for 'my' and is used when more than one person or thing belongs to you, whether they be masculine or feminine, for example, *mes frères* (my brothers); *mes sœurs* (my sisters); *mes crocodiles* (my crocodiles).

This is a tricky concept for most pupils to grasp as they naturally assume the word for 'my' is dependent on their own gender rather than that of the person or thing owned. It is important for pupils to understand that, even if a boy is speaking, he will still say *ma sœur* when talking about 'my sister'. The reverse is true of a girl talking about 'my brother' – *mon frère*.

Sœur
The 'œ' in *sœur* are joined together to show it is pronounced differently than other French words with 'oe'. Tell pupils not to worry about trying to join the letters when writing the word.

J'ai un frère

Sophie: Tu as des frères ou des sœurs, Nadine ?

Nadine: Oui, j'ai deux frères et une petite sœur. Elle a trois ans. Et toi ?

Sophie: J'ai un frère, mais je voudrais une sœur.

Luc: Salut !

Sophie & Nadine: Ah !

Nadine: C'est qui ?

Sophie: C'est mon frère. Il est bête ! Oh, je voudrais être enfant unique !

- -

J'ai un frère

Sophie: Tu as des frères ou des sœurs, Nadine ?

Nadine: Oui, j'ai deux frères et une petite sœur. Elle a trois ans. Et toi ?

Sophie: J'ai un frère, mais je voudrais une sœur.

Luc: Salut !

Sophie & Nadine: Ah !

Nadine: C'est qui ?

Sophie: C'est mon frère. Il est bête ! Oh, Je voudrais être enfant unique !

Voici ma famille

je m'appelle _____

J'ai une sœur et un frère,
J'ai une mère et un père.
Voici ma famille.

J'ai deux sœurs et un frère,
J'ai une mère et un père.
Voici ma famille.

J'ai une sœur et deux frères,
J'ai une mère et un père.
Voici ma famille.

J'ai deux sœurs et deux frères.
J'ai une mère et un père.
C'est une grande famille !

C'est mon biscuit ?

Write the correct word for 'my' in the blanks below.
Is it **mon**, **ma** or **mes**?

je m'appelle _____

Remember:
un = mon   une = ma   les/des = mes

1. _____ biscuit (un biscuit)

2. _____ poupée (une poupée)

3. _____ frère (un frère)

4. _____ sœur (une sœur)

5. _____ poupées (les/des poupées)

6. _____ biscuits (les/des biscuits)

Learn French with Luc et Sophie, Level 1
© Barbara Scanes and Brilliant Publications Limited

Tu as des frères ou des sœurs ?

Label these pictures with the correct sentence from the box at the bottom of the page.

je m'appelle _____

Par exemple:

J'ai un frère.

1.

2.

3.

4.

5.

J'ai deux frères.	J'ai une sœur.
Je suis enfant unique.	J'ai deux sœurs.
J'ai un frère.	J'ai un frère et une sœur.

Tu as des frères ou des sœurs ?

5e
Feuille de travail

Colour in the picture and write what you think Nadine is saying in the speech bubbles.

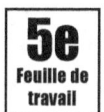

je m'appelle ______________________________

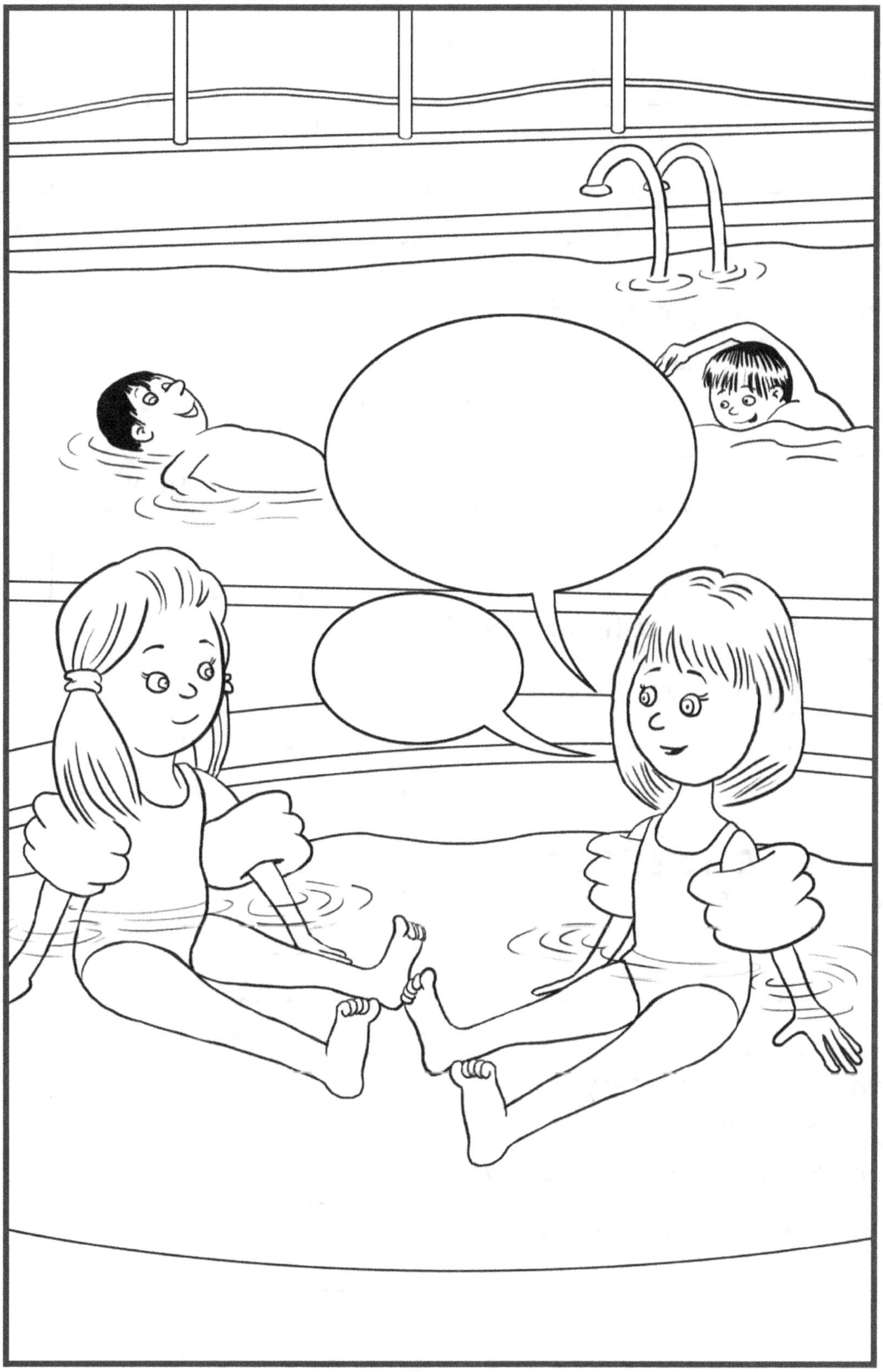

Self-assessment sheet
At the end of this unit I can...

Unité 5
Je peux...

je m'appelle _____

	date	not yet	nearly	definitely
understand when asked how many brothers and sisters I have				
say how many brothers and sisters I have				
ask someone else if they have brothers or sisters				

- -

Self-assessment sheet
At the end of this unit I can...

Unité 5
Je peux...

je m'appelle _____

	date	not yet	nearly	definitely
understand when asked how many brothers and sisters I have				
say how many brothers and sisters I have				
ask someone else if they have brothers or sisters				

- -

Self-assessment sheet
At the end of this unit I can...

Unité 5
Je peux...

je m'appelle _____

	date	not yet	nearly	definitely
understand when asked how many brothers and sisters I have				
say how many brothers and sisters I have				
ask someone else if they have brothers or sisters				

Beaucoup de bonbons

Unité 6

Cinq minutes français
Start the lesson, as usual, with greetings in French.

Revise asking/saying how many brothers and sisters you have by dividing the class into two and asking them to make a question chain (the first pupil asks the second who asks the third and so on until the last pupil asks the first and the chain is complete). Challenge them to see which half can finish their chain first while still pronouncing the words correctly.

Vocabulaire supplémentaire
Use actions to help explain your commands The additional vocabulary is modelled on Audio Track 36. (See also page 89 for more commands.)

Je vous divise en deux.	I'm dividing you into two.
Équipe A ici.	Team A here.
Et Équipe B là.	And Team B there.
(Pupil 1's name) *demande à* (Pupil 2's name), « *Tu as des frères ou des sœurs ?* »	(Pupil 1's name) asks (Pupil 2's name), 'Do you have any brothers or sisters?'
(Pupil 2's name) *répond.*	(Pupil 2's name) answers.
(Pupil 2's name) *demande à* (Pupil 3's name) …	(Pupil 2's name) asks (Pupil 3's name) …
Vous avez 30 secondes/une minute.	You have 30 seconds/1 minute. (Choose what you feel will work best with your class.)
Commencez !	Start!
Arrêtez !	Stop!

Vocabulaire
(Audio Track 34)

Sophie a	Sophie has
un bonbon	a sweet
des bonbons	some sweets
tu as combien de…?	how many… do you have?
onze	eleven
douze	twelve
treize	thirteen
quatorze	fourteen
quinze	fifteen
seize	sixteen
dix-sept	seventeen
dix-huit	eighteen
dix-neuf	nineteen
vingt	twenty
zéro	zero

Vocabulaire déjà utilisé

au revoir	goodbye
beaucoup de	lots of
je voudrais	I would like
mais	but
moi	me
non	no
pour	for
regardez	look
toi	you
tu as	you have

And numbers 1–10

Exercice 1 – Écouter
Play the story (Audio Track 33), pausing as necessary. Ask the pupils if they understood any of the story. Could they work out any of what was happening?

Exercice 2 – Écouter/lire

Display the audio enhanced e-storybook on the IWB. Click on the speech bubbles to hear what the characters are saying. Ask the pupils if they understand more now. Brainstorm the meaning of the entire story as a class-wide exercise. To hear the pronunciation of individual words/phrases, click on the words in the *Vocabulaire* lists on each page or in the *Vocabulaire* list at the end of the book.

Beaucoup de bonbons   Unité 6

 ### Exercice 3 – Chanter
Revise numbers to 10 with *La chanson des numéros* (the number song) (Audio Tracks 16 and 17). Listen carefully to the pronunciation of the numbers 11–20, using Audio Track 37. Pause after each number to allow pupils to repeat it after the speaker:

onze
douze
treize
quatorze
quinze
seize
dix-sept
dix-huit
dix-neuf
vingt

Sing the new number song on *Feuille* 6d and Audio Track 35. This song uses the same tune as the earlier number song but uses numbers up to 20 (instrumental Audio Track 17). Sing this song while counting on fingers (go back over the fingers for the numbers 11–20).

 ### Exercice 4 – Écouter
Ask the pupils to listen to Audio Track 38. Play each number and pause to enable the pupils to write down, in numeral form, the numbers they hear.

dix-huit
quinze
onze
dix-sept
vingt
quatorze
douze
seize
dix-neuf
treize

 ### Exercice 5 – Parler
Use the numeral flashcards (pages 43 and 73) to play a recognition game. As before, put pupils into pairs and ask one pupil to say the number in French in response to his/her partner showing a flashcard at random. They then swap places. You could also revise ages with the new numbers. Pupils should find this fun.

Vocabulaire pour le professeur
(Audio Track 36)

je vous divise en deux	I'm dividing you in two
équipe A ici et équipe B là	Team A here and Team B there
Sophie demande à Nadine : « Tu as des frères ou des sœurs ? »	Sophie asks Nadine, do have any brothers or sisters?'
Nadine répond	Nadine answers
vous avez 30 secondes	you have 30 seconds/
vous avez 1 minute	you have 1 minute
commencez	start
arrêtez	stop

Traduction de l'histoire

Lots of sweets
page 2
Hey! Look! Sophie has some sweets!
page 3
Sophie, I'd like a sweet!
And me!
And me!
page 4
No!
But you have lots of sweets!
No!
page 5
How many sweets do you have?
1, 2, 3, 4, 5, 6, 7, 8, 9, 10…
page 6
…11, 12, 13, 14, 15, 16, 17, 18, 19, 20.
So, four sweets for me, four for Henri, four for Luc, four for Nadine and four for Sophie.
page 7
No! Zero sweets for you, zero for Henri, zero for Luc, ten for Nadine and ten for me!
Goodbye!

Exercice 6 – Écouter

Play a 'Loto' (bingo) game. Ask pupils to write down five numbers at random between 0–20. Call out the numbers in French in random order until someone calls out *Loto!* They must then call back to you, in French, the numbers they have. This enables you to check their comprehension and them to practise saying the numbers. When the pupils have gained sufficient confidence with the numbers, you can ask them to take your place at calling out the numbers, although you may have to check they are saying the correct number.

Exercice 7 – Parler

This is an excellent 'starter' exercise for any lesson. Start with the first pupil in the class and ask that pupil to say *un*. The next pupil must say *deux* and so on until you reach *vingt*, whereupon start again with the next pupil in line with *un*.

A variation on this is to point, at random, to various pupils but they must still count sequentially. You can vary this game yet further by timing pupils with both variations and encouraging them to try to beat their best time.

A further variation is to divide the class into two sides and play 'number tennis'. Side A starts with *un* and side B then says *deux* and so on to twenty and then swap. You can speed this up to make it more challenging or ask the pupils to count in high voices, low voices, squeaky voices or sing the numbers! All of these variations provide ample practice at saying and learning the order of the numbers.

Exercice 8 – Parler

For this exercise you need to distribute numeral flashcards (pages 43 and 73) among the pupils. Each pupil needs a number, so you may have to photocopy and laminate more than one set. Give each pupil a flashcard. To begin with you can do this in the correct sequence. Ask each pupil to hold up their card and say their number loudly and in sequence. Time them and challenge them to improve their time.

Secondly, ask them to swap their number with anybody else in the room so that the cards are now out of sequence. Now ask the pupils to count sequentially again. This is more challenging since nobody will be sure who has the next number. The pupils need to be really on the ball with this one; be sure they know how to say their number (they can ask you before you commence if they are not sure) and to be ready to say it by listening carefully to the number sequence. Again, you can time them as a challenge and then swap number cards again.

Finally, to collect the flashcards in again, ask for the cards to be returned to you in reverse order, starting with *vingt* until they have given them all back in the correct order.

Exercice 9 – Lire

Play the game in *Exercice* 8 again with the pupils but, this time, use the flashcards bearing the name of the number (pages 44 and 74), not the numerals.

Feuille de travail

Feuilles de travail 6c and 6d reinforce the vocabulary learnt in the unit.

Grammaire

Avoir (to have)
In this story we meet the third person singular form of the verb *avoir* (to have): *Sophie **a** des bonbons*. We have previously met the first person singular form – *j'ai* and the second person singular form – *tu as*.

As we have already seen, *tu as* can become a question as well as a statement, purely by the addition of a question mark or, when spoken, by raising one's voice at the end of the sentence. The same is true for the third person, eg *Sophie a des bonbons ?* (Has Sophie got some sweets?)

Practise this form of the verb, both as a statement and question, with the following exercise. Use the names of children in your class and model the exercise yourself first by writing on the board, and then saying out loud, sentences such as:
- *Jake a un frère.*
- *Sarah a une sœur.*
- *Charlotte a sept ans.*
- *David a six ans.*

Check that your pupils understand what these sentences mean and then put some alternative endings on the board. If you have an interactive whiteboard it will be easy to colour code the parts of the sentence:

Subject	Verb	Object
Jake Sarah il elle mon frère ma sœur mon crocodile	*a*	un frère une sœur deux frères un crocodile dix ans vingt ans

Ask pupils to rearrange these to make different sentences which they will then read out loud. They can make these sentences as silly as they like as long as they are grammatically correct. Make the sentences into questions as well and turn this into a verbal exercise by asking your pupils, for example: *Jake a un crocodile ?*

A simple *non* or *oui* will suffice as an answer at this stage, although more ambitious or confident children might like to try an answer along the lines of: *non, mais il a dix sœurs*.

Beaucoup de bonbons

Luc: Eh! Regardez ! Sophie a des bonbons !

Luc: Sophie, je voudrais un bonbon !

Henri: Et moi !

Daniel: Et moi !

Sophie: Non!

Luc: Mais tu as beaucoup de bonbons !

Nadine: Non !

Henri: Tu as combien de bonbons ?

Sophie: Un, deux, trois, quatre, cinq, six, sept, huit, neuf, dix ...

Nadine: ... onze, douze, treize, quatorze, quinze, seize, dix-sept, dix-huit, dix-neuf, vingt.

Daniel: Alors, quatre bonbons pour moi, quatre pour Henri, quatre pour Luc, quatre pour Nadine

et quatre pour Sophie.

Sophie: Non! Zéro bonbons pour toi, zéro pour Henri,

zéro pour Luc, dix pour Nadine et dix pour

moi ! Au revoir !

La chanson des numéros

6b Chanson

Audio Tracks 35 & 17

je m'appelle _____

un,   deux,   trois,
1   **2**   **3**

quatre,   cinq,   six,
4   **5**   **6**

sept,   huit,   neuf et   dix.
7   **8**   **9**   **10**

onze,   douze,   treize,
11   **12**   **13**

quatorze,   quinze,   seize,
14   **15**   **16**

dix-sept,   dix-huit,   dix-neuf et   vingt.
17   **18**   **19**   **20**

Learn French with Luc et Sophie, Level 1
© Barbara Scanes and Brilliant Publications Limited

Tu as combien de bonbons ?

Write the correct number from the box below for the number of sweets in each picture.

je m'appelle _____

1. J'ai _____ bonbons.
2. J'ai _____ bonbons.
3. J'ai _____ bonbons.
4. J'ai _____ bonbons.
5. J'ai _____ bonbons.
6. J'ai _____ bonbons.
7. J'ai _____ bonbons.
8. J'ai _____ bonbons.
9. J'ai _____ bonbons.
10. J'ai _____ bonbons.

seize	vingt	quinze	quatorze	dix-huit
dix-sept	onze	treize	douze	beaucoup de

Learn French with Luc et Sophie, Level 1
© Barbara Scanes and Brilliant Publications Limited

Les bonbons

Colour in the picture and write what you think Nadine is saying in the speech bubble.

6d Feuille de travail

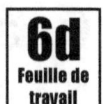

je m'appelle ______________________

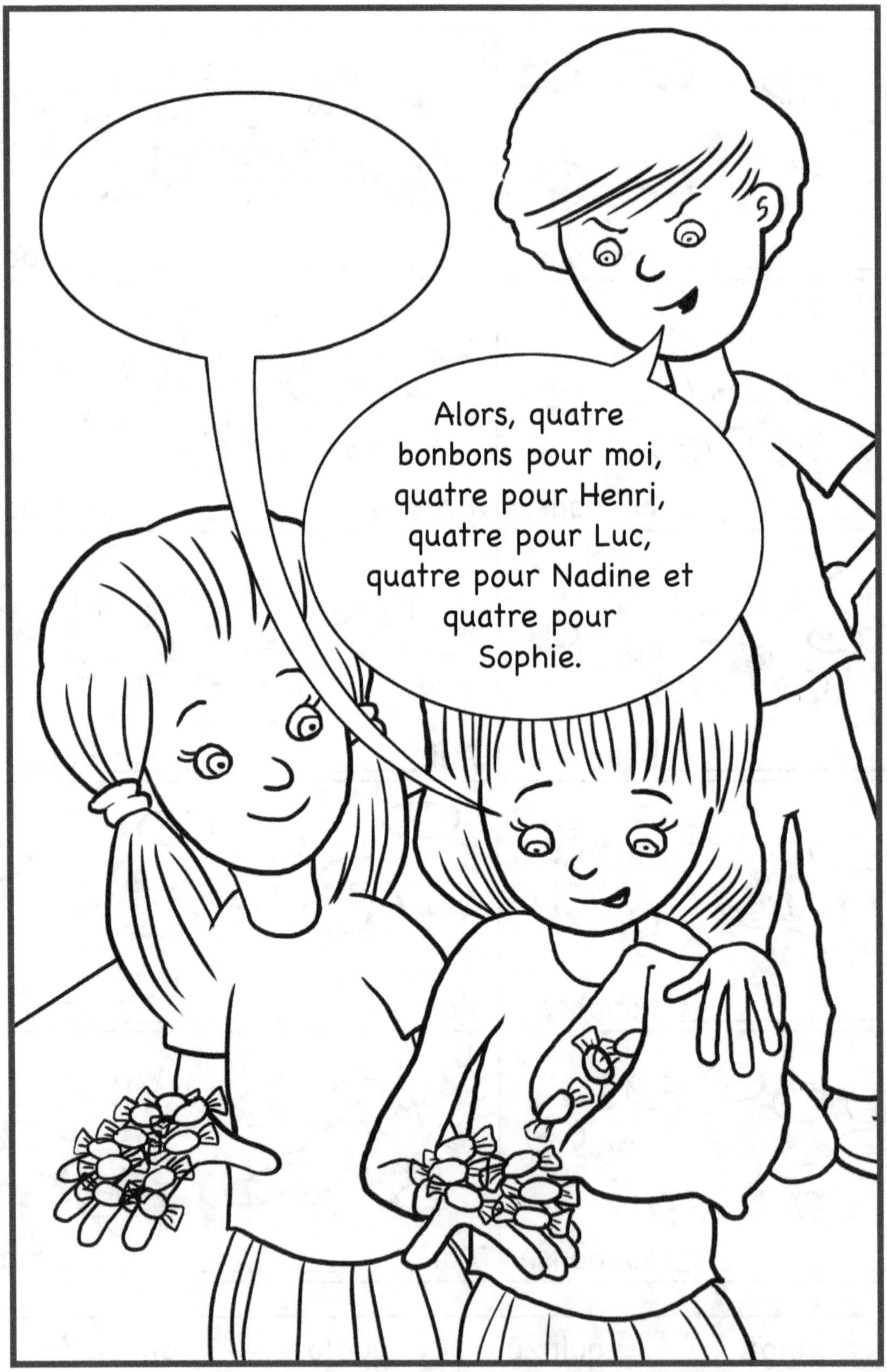

11	12
13	14
15	16
17	18
19	20

onze	douze
treize	quatorze
quinze	seize
dix-sept	dix-huit
dix-neuf	vingt

Self-assessment sheet
At the end of this unit I can...

Unité 6 Je peux...

je m'appelle _____

	date	not yet	nearly	definitely
recognise numbers to twenty				
count to twenty				
ask how many of something somebody has				
say I have lots of sweets				

- -

Self-assessment sheet
At the end of this unit I can...

Unité 6 Je peux...

je m'appelle _____

	date	not yet	nearly	definitely
recognise numbers to twenty				
count to twenty				
ask how many of something somebody has				
say I have lots of sweets				

- -

Self-assessment sheet
At the end of this unit I can...

Unité 6 Je peux...

je m'appelle _____

	date	not yet	nearly	definitely
recognise numbers to twenty				
count to twenty				
ask how many of something somebody has				
say I have lots of sweets				

Un bonbon rouge

Unité 7

 Cinq minutes français
Begin the lesson with greetings in French and playing the *Ça va ?* game (see *Unité 2, Exercice 4*).

Revise numbers to 20 with *La chanson des numéros* (Audio Tracks 35 and 17), counting on fingers. Use the command: *Maintenant, chantez !* (Now sing!)

Revise ages using flashcards. Show a numeral flashcard between 1–20 (pages 43 and 73) and ask a child: *Quel âge as-tu ?* They should answer *j'ai … ans* depending on the number on the card. If there is time, hand out a card to each child and ask them to ask each other.

 Exercice 1 – Écouter
Play the story (Audio Track 39), pausing as necessary. Ask the pupils if they understood any of the story. Could they work out any of what was happening?

 Exercice 2 – Écouter/lire

Display the audio enhanced e-storybook on the IWB. Click on the speech bubbles to hear what the characters are saying. Ask the pupils if they understand more now. Brainstorm the meaning of the entire story as a class-wide exercise. To hear the pronunciation of individual words/phrases, click on the words in the *Vocabulaire* lists on each page or in the *Vocabulaire* list at the end of the book.

 Exercice 3 – Écouter
Play the listening exercise on Audio Track 44:

bleu
rouge
vert
orange
jaune
rose
violet
marron

Ask the pupils to repeat each colour after the speaker. Next, ask children to guess which colour is which. Ask: *C'est quelle couleur ?* (What colour is it?) They will probably guess *bleu* and *orange*. Point out the different pronunciation of *orange*. Ask the children to think about the difference in sound between *bleu* and 'blue'.

Vocabulaire
(Audio Track 40)

seul	only/alone
rouge	red
bleu	blue
vert	green
jaune	yellow
orange	orange
rose	pink
violet	purple
marron	brown
fermez les yeux	close your eyes
ouvrez les yeux	open your eyes
gagner	to win
devinez	guess
la couleur	the colour
qui manque	which is missing
c'est le rouge	it's the red (one)
c'est nul	it's rubbish/that's rubbish

Vocabulaire déjà utilisé

écoutez	listen
un bonbon	a sweet
j'ai	I have
moi	me
maman	mum
non	no
pour	for

Play Track 44 again. This time show the appropriate colour flashcard (page 85) for each colour mentioned as you hear it. (Note: you will find a colour version in the Digital Downloads. If you are photocopying the page from the book you will need to colour in the splodges with the different colours.)

On the third playing of the track, pause the track after each colour is mentioned and ask the children to repeat it while you show the correct colour flashcard.

Vocabulaire pour le professeur
(Audio Track 43)

c'est quelle couleur ?	what colour is it?
les couleurs	the colours
devinez la couleur qui manque	guess the colour that's missing
c'est le vert	it's the green (one)
montrez-moi quelque chose de bleu	show me something that's blue

 ## Exercice 4 – Parler
Show each colour flashcard one at a time and ask the pupils to tell you the French name for the colour, with the question: *C'est quelle couleur ?* (What colour is it?) After you have shown all the flashcards, change the order and go round again.

Next time, choose a pupil to come to the front. Ask the pupil to select a colour flashcard and ask the class, *C'est quelle couleur ?* The pupil with the flashcard can choose another pupil to answer the question and, if it is answered correctly and with correct pronunciation, the second pupil comes to the front and takes a turn. Ensure that all the colours are covered.

Traduction de l'histoire

A red sweet
page 2
Sophie! Nadine! Only one sweet, then, please!
Listen, I have a red sweet, a blue sweet, a green sweet and a yellow sweet.
page 3
I have an orange sweet, a pink sweet, a purple sweet and a brown sweet.
Now, shut your eyes!
page 4
Open your eyes! To win a sweet, guess which colour is missing!
page 5
It's the red one!
No!
page 6
It's the brown one!
No!
It's the green one!
No!
page 7
Oh, that's rubbish!
Ow! Mum!

 ## Exercice 5 – Parler
Put pupils into pairs. One pupil shows his/her partner an item (eg a crayon or book) in one of the eight colours and asks: *C'est quelle couleur ?* The partner must respond with the correct French name for the colour and then swaps and becomes the questioner.

Exercice 6 – Lire
Use the word flashcards (page 86) to introduce pupils to the spelling of the French names for colours. Show pupils each card and ask them to repeat the name of the colour after you. Highlight the difference in the spelling between *bleu* and 'blue'. Can they think why they are so similar? ('blue' derives from the French word, *bleu*). Also, look at how *orange* has the same spelling as in English but the pronunciation is quite different.

 ## Exercice 7 – Écrire
Put pupils into pairs. They spell out the name of a colour in French with 'air writing' and/or writing on their partner's back and take it in turns to guess the correct colour.

Exercice 8 – Écouter
Play a game where pupils must find something in the classroom of the colour you name in French. *Montrez-moi quelque chose de bleu* (Show me something blue.) Challenge the pupils to find as many different things as possible in each colour.

Exercice 9 – Écrire
Ask pupils to make a poster of the eight colours with the title *Les couleurs*. Remind pupils to write *je m'appelle ...* at the top of the poster. They could draw different coloured shapes and label them with the correct French name, or some objects from nature – flowers, trees, the sun – in the different colours and label these with their French name.

Exercice 10 – Écouter
Listen to Audio Track 45. This listening exercise introduces two new instructions, *Fermez les yeux !* (close your eyes) and *Ouvrez les yeux !* (open your eyes), and refreshes those already encountered in Unit 1.

Fermez les yeux !
Ouvrez les yeux !
Regardez !
Écoutez !
Levez-vous !

Play Audio Track 45 again and this time ask the pupils to make the appropriate action for the instruction heard. Play the game again, choosing different pupils to lead the game, choosing a different instruction each time.

Exercice 11 – Écouter
Practise the instruction *devinez* (guess) using the colour flashcards. Show the pupils all eight flashcards and revise the colours orally with them. Instruct the pupils *Fermez les yeux !* and hide one of the colour flashcards behind your back. Instruct the pupils *Ouvrez les yeux !* and say to them *devinez la couleur qui manque*. The pupil who says the correct missing colour with the correct phrase, eg *c'est le vert* gets to lead the next game.

Exercice 12 – Chanter
Teach the song *Un bonbon bleu* to reinforce the vocabulary (*Feuille* 7b), Audio Tracks 41 and 42 (instrumental version).

Feuilles de travail
Feuilles de travail 7c, 7d and 7e reinforce the vocabulary learnt in the unit.

Grammaire

Colours in French
Ask pupils if they have noticed where the colour adjective goes in the sentence. In English we put the colour adjective **before** the noun but in French it goes **after.**
eg a blue sweet = *un bonbon bleu*

This is true of nearly all adjectives in French.

Adjectives in French will also change their spelling, and sometimes also their pronunciation, according to whether they are describing a feminine or masculine noun. This grammatical point will be explored in more detail in later levels. For now, please ensure that children only use masculine nouns if they want to describe them with a colour. See the vocabulary boxes and *Vocabulaire* (pages 92–93) for gender.

Also note that, in the story, *le rouge* is used to mean 'the red **one**'. The word 'one' is implied rather than explicitly stated and '*le*' is used as it refers to *le bonbon*. If a feminine noun were being referred to, eg *la fleur* (the flower), then 'the red one' would be translated as *la rouge*.

Un bonbon rouge

7a Petite pièce

Luc: Sophie ! Nadine ! Un seul bonbon, alors, s'il vous plaît !

Sophie: Écoutez, j'ai un bonbon rouge, un bonbon bleu, un bonbon vert et un bonbon jaune.

Nadine: Et moi, j'ai un bonbon orange, un bonbon rose, un bonbon violet et un bonbon marron.

Sophie: Alors, fermez les yeux !

Sophie: Ouvrez les yeux ! Pour gagner un bonbon, devinez la couleur qui manque !

Luc: C'est le rouge !

Sophie: Non !

Henri: C'est le marron !

Nadine: Non !

Daniel: C'est le vert !

Sophie: Non !

Luc: Ah, c'est nul !

Sophie: Ouah ! Maman !

Un bonbon bleu

je m'appelle _____

Je voudrais un bonbon bleu,

Un bonbon rouge,

Un bonbon vert.

Je voudrais un bonbon bleu !

Non, non, non !

Je voudrais un bonbon rose,

Violet

Ou orange.

Je voudrais un bonbon rose !

Non, non, non !

Je voudrais un bonbon jaune,

Rose ou marron

Ou orange.

Je voudrais un bonbon rouge !

Ah, c'est nul !

Colour the sweets the correct colour.

C'est quelle couleur ?

Unscramble the colours and then draw something in the correct colour in the box.

je m'appelle _____

1. elub	2. ores
3. ugore	4. trev
5. romarn	6. neuja
7. olivet	8. rangeo

Les couleurs

Colour the picture in the correct colours, using the key below.
Where there isn't a number, choose your own colour.

je m'appelle _____

1	=	rouge	5 =	bleu
2	=	jaune	6 =	marron
3	=	orange	7 =	rose
4	=	vert	8 =	violet

Learn French with Luc et Sophie, Level 1

C'est quelle couleur ?

Colour in the picture and write what you think Nadine is saying in the speech bubbles.

je m'appelle _____

7e
Feuille de travail

Un bonbon rouge

Unité 7

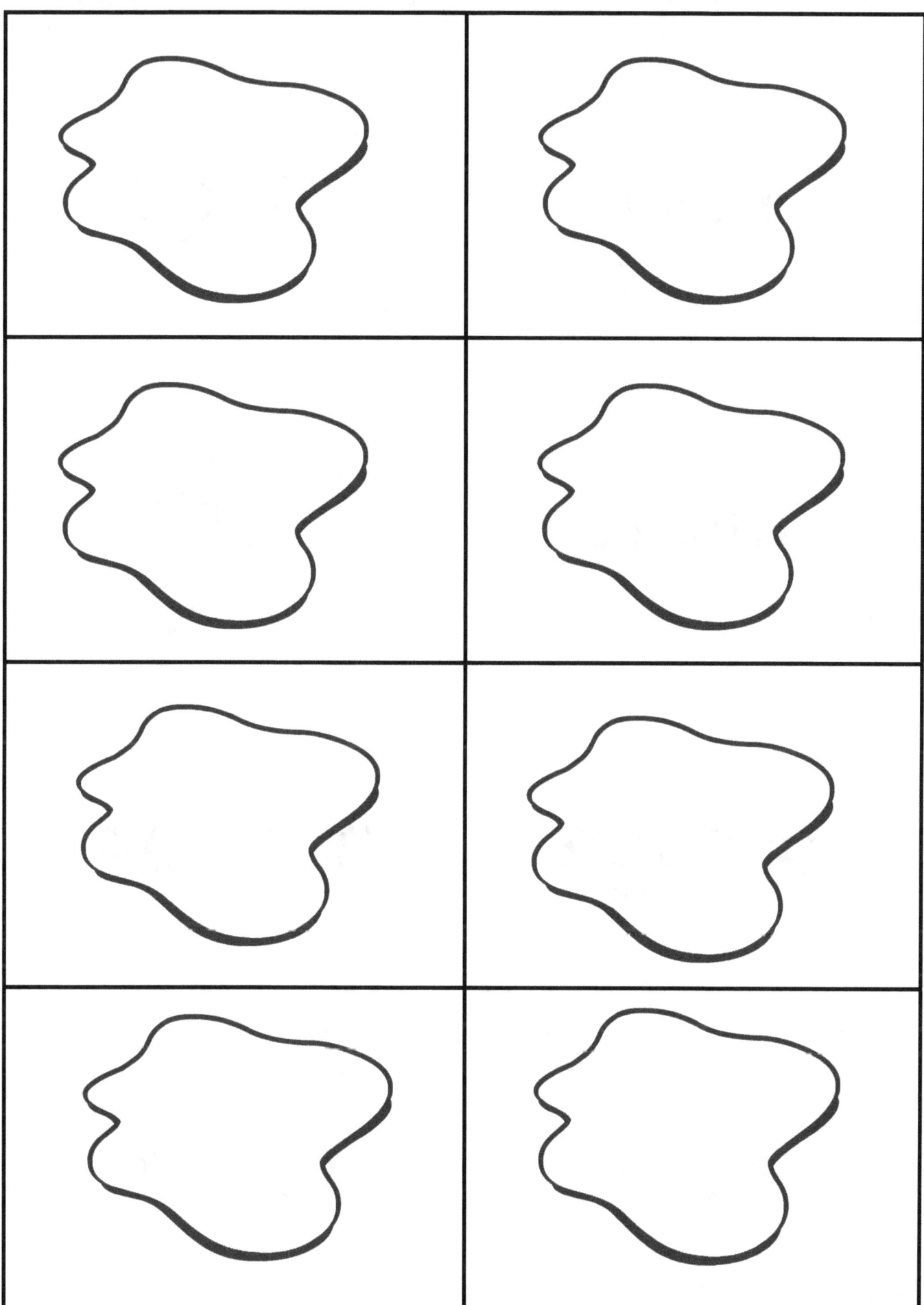

Learn French with Luc et Sophie, Level 1

bleu	rouge
jaune	vert
orange	marron
rose	violet

Self-assessment sheet
At the end of this unit I can...

Unité 7 Je peux...

je m'appelle _____

	date	not yet	nearly	definitely
recognise the name of eight colours in French				
say the name of eight colours in French				
understand and respond to five commands				

- -

Self-assessment sheet
At the end of this unit I can...

Unité 7 Je peux...

je m'appelle _____

	date	not yet	nearly	definitely
recognise the name of eight colours in French				
say the name of eight colours in French				
understand and respond to five commands				

- -

Self-assessment sheet
At the end of this unit I can...

Unité 7 Je peux...

je m'appelle _____

	date	not yet	nearly	definitely
recognise the name of eight colours in French				
say the name of eight colours in French				
understand and respond to five commands				

Traductions des chansons (Song translations)

Unité 1
Mum says

Mum says 'Good morning Luc!'
Silence, silence, silence.
Mum says 'Good morning Luc!'
Silence, silence, silence.

Mum says 'Good morning Sophie!'
Silence, silence, silence.
Mum says 'Good morning Sophie!'
Silence, silence, silence.

Mum says 'Listen!'
Silence, silence, silence.
Mum says 'Listen!'
Silence, silence, silence.

Mum says 'Look!
A croco- crocodile!'
Mum says 'Look!
A croco- crocodile!'

Mum says 'It's me, it's me,
So get up!'.
Mum says 'It's me, it's me,
So get up!'

Unité 2
Hello, how are you?

Hello, how are you?
What's your name?
My name is Hervé
And I'm fine.

Hello, how are you?
What's your name?
My name is Élodie
And yes, I'm OK.

Hello, how are you?
What's your name?
My name is Serge
And I'm well, thank you.

Hello, how are you?
What's your name?
My name is Mireille
And I'm not well.

Goodbye!

Unité 3
One biscuit, two biscuits

One biscuit, two biscuits, three biscuits for you.
Four biscuits, five biscuits, six biscuits for me.
Seven biscuits, eight biscuits for my nine dolls.
Ten biscuits? Ten biscuits! Oh yes – look!

Unité 4
How old are you?

How old are you? I'm five.
No, you're four!
How old are you? I'm six.
Yes, you're six.

How old are you? I'm seven.
No, you're six!
How old are you? I'm eight.
Yes, you're eight.

How old are you? I'm nine.
No, you're seven!
How old are you? I'm ten.
Yes, you're ten.

How old are you? I'm eleven.
No, you're ten!
It's nearly my birthday!
And I will be eleven.
Or perhaps you will be
A hundred years old like an elephant!

Unité 5
Here is my family

I have a sister and a brother.
I have a mother and a father.
Here is my family.

I have two sisters and a brother.
I have a mother and a father.
Here is my family.

I have a sister and two brothers.
I have a mother and a father.
Here is my family.

I have two sisters and two brothers.
I have a mother and a father.
It's a big family!

Unité 6
The numbers song

One, two, three
Four, five, six
Seven, eight, nine and ten.

Eleven, twelve, thirteen,
Fourteen, fifteen, sixteen,
Seventeen, eighteen, nineteen and twenty.

Unité 7
A blue sweet

I would like a blue sweet,
A red sweet
A green sweet.
I would like a blue sweet,
No, no, no!

I would like a pink sweet,
A purple one
Or an orange one.
I would like a pink sweet,
No, no, no!

I would like a yellow sweet,
A pink or brown one
Or an orange one
I would like a red sweet,
Oh, that's rubbish!

Instructions utiles (Useful commands)

Plural (Audio Track 46)	Singular (Audio Track 47)	English
Levez-vous	Lève-toi	Stand up
Asseyez-vous	Assieds-toi	Sit down
Levez le doigt	Lève le doigt	Raise your hand (literally: raise your finger)
Baissez le doigt	Baisse le doigt	Lower your hand (literally: lower your finger)
Fermez …	Ferme …	Close …
Fermez les yeux	Ferme les yeux	Close your eyes
Fermez la porte	Ferme la porte	Close the door
Fermez le livre	Ferme le livre	Close the book
Ouvrez …	Ouvre …	Open …
Ouvrez les yeux	Ouvre les yeux	Open your eyes
Ouvrez le cahier	Ouvre le cahier	Open the exercise book
Ouvrez la fenêtre	Ouvre la fenêtre	Open the window
Arrêtez	Arrête	Stop
Allez au tableau blanc	Va au tableau blanc	Go to the whiteboard
Chantez	Chante	Sing
Chuchotez	Chuchote	Whisper
Répétez …	Répète …	Repeat …
Répétez d'une voix aiguë	Répète d'une voix aiguë	Repeat in a squeaky voice
Répétez d'une voix basse	Répète d'une voix basse	Repeat in a low voice
Répétez d'une voix forte	Répète d'une voix forte	Repeat in a loud voice
Faites comme moi	Fais comme moi	Copy me
Montrez-moi	Montre-moi	Show me
Dites-moi	Dis-moi	Tell me
Travaillez …		Work …
Travaillez à deux		Work in pairs
Travaillez à trois		Work in threes
Travaillez à quatre		Work in fours
Travaillez en groupe		Work as a group
Lisez	Lis	Read
Coloriez	Colorie	Colour
Écrivez	Écris	Write
Dessinez	Dessine	Draw
Sortez du jeu	Sors du jeu	Leave the game/you're out!

Les téléchargements numériques (Digital downloads)

Audio enhanced e-storybooks

Unit no.	File name in free digital downloads	
1	LFLS1-1-ESTORY-PP.ppsx	Bonjour
2	LFLS1-2-ESTORY-PP.ppsx	Je m'appelle Sophie
3	LFLS1-3-ESTORY-PP.ppsx	Combien de biscuits ?
4	LFLS1-4-ESTORY-PP.ppsx	J'ai six ans
5	LFLS1-5-ESTORY-PP.ppsx	J'ai un frère
6	LFLS1-6-ESTORY-PP.ppsx	Beaucoup de bonbons
7	LFLS1-7-ESTORY-PP.ppsx	Un bonbon rouge

Audio files

Track no.	File name in free digital downloads	
Unité 1		
1	LFLS1-1-AUDIO.mp3	Story – Bonjour
2	LFLS1-2-AUDIO.mp3	Vocabulaire
3	LFLS1-3-AUDIO.mp3	Song – Maman dit
4	LFLS1-4-AUDIO.mp3	Instrumental for song – Maman dit
5	LFLS1-5-AUDIO.mp3	Vocabulaire pour le professeur
Unité 2		
6	LFLS1-6-AUDIO.mp3	Story – *Je m'appelle Sophie*
7	LFLS1-7-AUDIO.mp3	*Vocabulaire*
8	LFLS1-8-AUDIO.mp3	Song – *Bonjour, ça va ?*
9	LFLS1-9-AUDIO.mp3	Instrumental for song – *Bonjour, ça va ?*
10	LFLS1-10-AUDIO.mp3	*Vocabulaire pour le professeur*
11	LFLS1-11-AUDIO.mp3	*Exercice* 6 – French names
Unité 3		
12	LFLS1-12-AUDIO.mp3	Story – Combien de biscuits ?
13	LFLS1-13-AUDIO.mp3	Vocabulaire
14	LFLS1-14-AUDIO.mp3	Song – Un biscuit, deux biscuits
15	LFLS1-15-AUDIO.mp3	Instrumental for song – Un biscuit, deux biscuits
16	LFLS1-16-AUDIO.mp3	Song – La chanson des numéros (version 1)
17	LFLS1-17AUDIO.mp3	Instrumental for song – La chanson des numéros
18	LFLS1-18-AUDIO.mp3	Vocabulaire pour le professeur
19	LFLS1-19-AUDIO.mp3	Exercice 6 – numbers 1–10 (mixed up)
Unité 4		
20	LFLS1-20-AUDIO.mp3	Story – J'ai six ans
21	LFLS1-21-AUDIO.mp3	Vocabulaire
22	LFLS1-22-AUDIO.mp3	Song – Quel âge as-tu ?

23	LFLS1-23-AUDIO.mp3	Instrumental for song – Quel âge as-tu ?
24	LFLS1-24-AUDIO.mp3	Vocabulaire pour le professeur
25	LFLS1-25-AUDIO.mp3	Exercice 5 – ages 1–10 (in order)
26	LFLS1-26-AUDIO.mp3	Exercice 5 – ages 1–10 (mixed up)
Unité 5		
27	LFLS1-27-AUDIO.mp3	Story – J'ai un frère
28	LFLS1-28-AUDIO.mp3	Vocabulaire
29	LFLS1-29-AUDIO.mp3	Song – Voici ma famille
30	LFLS1-30-AUDIO.mp3	Instrumental for song – Voici ma famille
31	LFLS1-31-AUDIO.mp3	Vocabulaire pour le professeur
32	LFLS1-32-AUDIO.mp3	Exercice 4 – brothers and sisters
Unité 6		
33	LFLS1-33-AUDIO.mp3	Story – Beaucoup de bonbons
34	LFLS1-34-AUDIO.mp3	Vocabulaire
35	LFLS1-35-AUDIO.mp3	Song – La chanson des numéros (version 2)
36	LFLS1-36-AUDIO.mp3	Vocabulaire pour le professeur
37	LFLS1-37-AUDIO.mp3	Exercice 3 – numbers 11–20 (in order)
38	LFLS1-38-AUDIO.mp3	Exercice 4 – numbers 11–20 (mixed up)
Unité 7		
39	LFLS1-39-AUDIO.mp3	Story – Un bonbon rouge
40	LFLS1-40-AUDIO.mp3	Vocabulaire
41	LFLS1-41-AUDIO.mp3	Song – Un bonbon bleu
42	LFLS1-42-AUDIO.mp3	Instrumental for song – Un bonbon bleu
43	LFLS1-43-AUDIO.mp3	Vocabulaire pour le professeur
44	LFLS1-44-AUDIO.mp3	Exercice 3 – colours
45	LFLS1-45-AUDIO.mp3	Exercice 10 – commands
Pour le professeur (for the teacher)		
46	LFLS1-46-AUDIO.mp3	Instructions utiles (useful commands) – plural
47	LFLS1-47-AUDIO.mp3	Instructions utiles (useful commands) – singular

Printable resources		
PDF versions of storybooks		
Unit no.	File name in free digital downloads	
1	LFLS1-1-STORY-PDF.pdf	Bonjour
2	LFLS1-2-STORY-PDF.pdf	Je m'appelle Sophie
3	LFLS1-3-STORY-PDF.pdf	Combien de biscuits ?
4	LFLS1-4-STORY-PDF.pdf	J'ai six ans
5	LFLS1-5-STORY-PDF.pdf	J'ai un frère
6	LFLS1-6-STORY-PDF.pdf	Beaucoup de bonbons
7	LFLS1-7-STORY-PDF.pdf	Un bonbon rouge
PDF versions of worksheets		
	LFLS1-RESOURCES-PDF.pdf	

Vocabulaire (Vocabulary)

Note: the Unité column indicates the unit where the word is first introduced. Where there is (P) in brackets, this indicates that the word was 'Vocabulaire supplémentaire pour le professeur' and not used in the story. The Track number column indicates the vocabulary track where you can hear the word pronounced by a native French speaker.

Definite or indefinite articles have been given for all nouns to reinforce that they are needed in French. They have been translated literally into English. However, please use your discretion and the context when deciding whether to include these articles when translating the nouns into English.

French	English	Unité	Track no.
alors	so, then	1	2
alors, maintenant chantez !	now sing!	5 (P)	31
mon anniversaire	my birthday	4	21
arrêtez	stop (plural/formal)	6 (P)	36
au revoir	good bye	2	7
avoir	to have (see page 93)	6 (P)	–
beaucoup (de)	lots (of)	3	13
un beau-père	(a) step father	5 (P)	31
un bébé	(a) baby	4	21
une belle-mère	(a) step mother	5 (P)	31
bête	silly	5	28
bien	well/fine	2	7
bientôt	soon	4	21
un biscuit	(a) biscuit	3	13
des biscuits	(some) biscuits	3	13
bleu	blue	7	40
un bonbon	(a) sweet	6	34
des bonbons	(some) sweets	6	34
bonjour	good morning/hello	1	2
ça va	I'm fine/things are fine	2	7
ça va ?	how are you?/are you OK?/how are things?	2	7
ça va bien, merci	I'm very well, thank you	2	7
ça va mal	I'm not well/things are bad	2	7
c'est	it is	4	21
c'est le rouge	it's the red (one)	7	40
c'est le vert	it's the green (one)	7 (P)	43
c'est moi	it's me	1	2
c'est nul	it's rubbish/that's rubbish	7	40
c'est quelle couleur ?	what colour is it?	7 (P)	43
c'est qui ?	who is that?/who is it?	5	28
cinq	five	3	13
cinq minutes français	5 minutes of French	2 (P)	10
combien (de) ?	how many?	3	13
combien de biscuits ?	how many biscuits?	3	13
comme	like	4 (P)	24
commencez	start (plural/formal)	6 (P)	36
comment t'appelles-tu ?	what's your name? (singular/informal)	2	7
la couleur	(the) colour	7	40
les couleurs	(the) colours	7 (P)	43
un crocodile	crocodile	1	2
un demi-frère	(a) half brother/step-brother	5 (P)	31
une demi-sœur	(a) half sister/step-sister	5 (P)	31
deux	two	3	13
devinez	guess (plural/formal)	7	40
devinez la couleur qui manque	guess the colour that's missing	7 (P)	43
dix	ten	3	13
dix-huit	eighteen	6	34
dix-neuf	nineteen	6	34
dix-sept	seventeen	6	34
douze	twelve	6	34
écoutez	listen (plural/formal)	1	2
un éléphant	an elephant	4 (P)	24
elle a trois ans	she is three (years old)	5	28
en ce moment	at the moment	4	21
un enfant unique	(an) only child	5	28
les enfants	(the) children	3 (P)	18
équipe A ici	Team A here	6 (P)	36
et équipe B là	and Team B there	6 (P)	36
et toi ?	and you?	2	7
être	to be (see page 94)	5	28
ma famille	my family	5 (P)	31
ma grande famille	my big family	5 (P)	31
fermez les yeux	close your eyes (formal/plural)	7	40
un frère	(a) brother	5	28
des frères	(some) brothers	5	28
deux frères	two brothers	5	28
mon frère	my brother	5	28
gagner	to win	7	40

huit	eight	3	13
il est	he is	5	28
ils sont	they are	3	13
Jacques a dit	Jack said	1 (P)	5
jaune	yellow	7	40
j'ai	I have	3	13
j'ai six ans	I'm six (years old)	4	21
j'aurai	I will have (j'aurai 10 ans = I will be 10 years old)	4 (P)	24
je m'appelle …	my name is…	2	7
je suis	I am	5 (P)	31
je voudrais	I would like	5	28
je vous divise en deux	I'm dividing you in two	6 (P)	36
levez-vous	get up (plural/formal)	1	2
madame	Mrs/'Miss' (at school)	3 (P)	18
maintenant, comptez en français	now count in French	4 (P)	24
mais	but	3	13
maman	mum	1	2
maman arrive	mum's coming	2	7
maman dit	Mum says	1 (P)	5
marron	brown	7	40
une mère	(a) mother	5 (P)	31
moi	me	3	13
monsieur	Mr/'Sir' (at school)	3 (P)	18
montrez-moi quelque chose de bleu	show me something that's blue (plural/formal)	7 (P)	43
neuf	nine	3	13
non	no	1	2
onze	eleven	4(P)/6	34
orange	orange	7	40
ou	or	5	28
oui	yes	3	13
ouvrez les yeux	open your eyes (formal/plural)	7	40
un père	(a) father	5 (P)	31
peut-être	maybe	4 (P)	24
mes poupées	my dolls	3	13
pour	for	3	13
quatorze	fourteen	6	34
quatre	four	3	13
quel âge as-tu ?	how old are you?	4	21
qui manque	which is missing	7	40
quinze	fifteen	6	34
regardez	look (plural/formal)	1	2
rose	pink	7	40
rouge	red	7	40
salut	hi (or bye)	3	13
seize	sixteen	6	34
sept	seven	3	13
seul	only/alone	7	40
s'il vous plaît	please (plural/formal)	1	2
silence	silence	1 (P)	5
six	six	3	13
une sœur	a sister	5	28
des sœurs	(some) sisters	5	28
une petite sœur	(a) little sister	5	28
Sophie a	Sophie has	6	34
treize	thirteen	6	34
trois	three	3	13
tu as	you have	3	13
tu as ?	have you (got)?	5	28
tu as combien de … ?	how many … do you have?	6	34
tu as sept ans	you're seven (years old)	4	21
tu as sept ans ?	Are you seven (years old)?	4	21
tu (en) auras	you will have (tu auras 10 ans = you will be 10 years old)	4 (P)	24
tu es	you are	4	21
tu sors du jeu	you're out (singular/informal)	2 (P)	10
un	one	3	13
vert	green	7	40
vingt	twenty	6	34
violet	purple	7	40
voici	here (is)	5(P)	31
vous avez 30 secondes/1 minute	you have 30 seconds/1 minute (plural/formal)	6 (P)	36
X demande à Y : « Tu as des frères ou des sœurs ? »	X asks Y, 'do you have any brothers or sisters?'	6 (P)	36
Y répond	Y answers	6 (P)	36
zéro	zero	6	34

How to conjugate *avoir* in the present tense:

j'ai	I have
tu as	you have (singular/informal)
il a	he has
elle a	she has
nous avons	we have
vous avez	you have (plural/formal)
ils ont	they have (males or mixture of males and females)
elles ont	they have (females only)

How to conjugate *être* in the present tense:

je suis	I am
tu es	you are (singular/informal)
il est	he is
elle est	she is
nous sommes	we are
vous êtes	you are (plural/formal)
ils sont	they are (males or mixture of males and females)
elles sont	they are (females only)

Solutions (Answers)

Feuilles de travail

Feuille de travail 1c – page 20

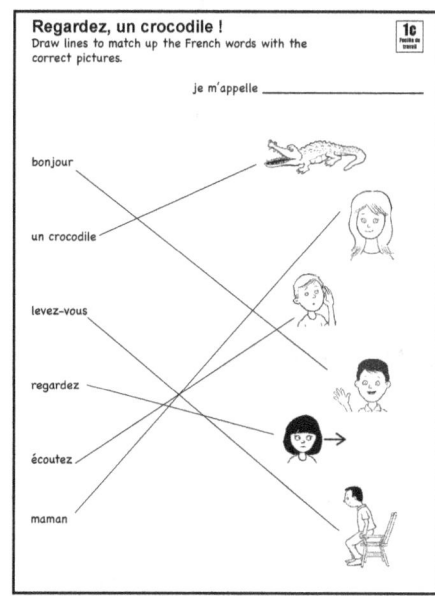

Feuille de travail 2c – page 29
1. Ça va
2. Ça va bien
3. Ça va ?
4. Ça val mal

(Note: accept pupils' answers if they give logical explanations for their choices)

Feuille de travail 2d – page 30
1. Je m'appelle Marc.
2. Bonjour ! Je m'appelle Sophie.
3. Ça va ?
4. Comment t'appelles-tu ?
5. Au revoir !

Feuille de travail 3c – page 40
1. deux
2. huit
3. quatre
4. neuf
5. un
6. sept
7. six
8. cinq

Feuille de travail 3d – page 41

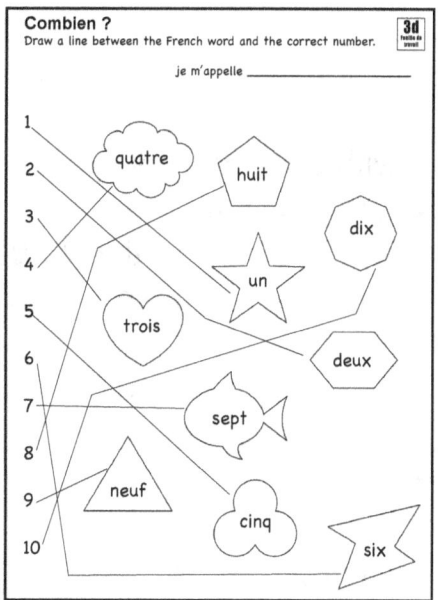

Feuille de travail 4c – page 51
1. Sophie – six
2. Nadine – cinq
3. Luc – sept
4. neuf
5. trois

Feuille de travail 5c – page 61
1. mon biscuit
2. ma poupée
3. mon frère
4. ma sœur
5. mes poupées
6. mes biscuits

Feuille de travail 5d – page 62
1. J'ai une sœur.
2. J'ai deux frères.
3. J'au un frère and une sœur.
4. J'ai deux sœurs.
5. Je suis enfant unique.

Feuille de travail 6c - page 71
1. treize
2. vingt
3. onze
4. seize
5. quinze
6. dix-huit
7. quatorze
8. douze
9. dix-sept
10. beaucoup de

Feuille de travail 7c – page 82
1. bleu
2. rose
3. rouge
4. vert
5. marron
6. jaune
7. violet
8. orange

Learn French with Luc et Sophie, Level 1
© Barbara Scanes and Brilliant Publications Limited

Instructions for downloading the free digital files

To download your free resources for **Learn French with Luc et Sophie, Level 1**:

Go to: https://www.brilliantpublications.education

You will need to set up a log in with an email address and password if you do not already have one for the https://www.brilliantpublications.education website. (Please note: you will need to set up a new account on this website to download your files, even if you already have an account on our main website.)

Your username may contain: letters, numbers and the special characters * - _ . @
You will be asked to confirm your email address by clicking the validation link emailed to you when you register.

Don't forget to check in spam/junk if you do not see an email from us.

We have introduced 2-factor authorisation on this website to make it more secure. This means that whenever you log in, you will be sent a numerical authorisation code by email which you must copy and paste into the welcome page on the website. The authentication code only lasts 1 hour.

Once logged on, choose the '**French**' category and click on the cover for **Learn French with Luc et Sophie, Level 1**.

Your unique password for the downloads is: **Pm70m91YH**

The downloaded filename will be **Luc-et-Sophie-Level-1.zip**

Please note, the password will be changed at regular intervals so make sure you save a copy of the files once you have downloaded them.

If you experience any difficulties with downloading your files, please email info@brilliantpublications.co.uk and we will get back to you as soon as possible.

Depending on the speed of your internet and the size of the download, it may take some time for the download to complete. To avoid problems, please make sure that your computer does not go to sleep during the download.

Note: We test the software on PCs and Apple Macs, but there are too many different types of hardware in schools for us to be able to test it on every device owned by schools.